brave brave brave brave brave brave bra
brave brave brave brave brave brave brave
ave brave bra brave brave bra
brave brave b brave brave
ave brave bra ve brave bra
brave brave brave brave brave brave brave
ave brave brave brave brave brave brave bra
brave brave brave brave brave brave brave
ave brave brave brave brave brave brave bra
brave brave brave brave brave brave brave
ave brave brave brave brave brave brave bra
brave brave brave brave brave brave brave
ave brave brave brave brave brave brave bra
brave brave brave brave brave brave brave
ave brave brave brave brave brave brave bra
brave brave brave brave brave brave brave
ave brave brave brave brave brave brave bra
brave brave brave brave brave brave brave

brave brave brave brave brave brave brave
ave brave brave brave brave brave brave bra
brave brave brave brave brave brave brave
ave brave brave brave brave brave brave bra
brave brave brave brave brave brave brave
ave brave brave brave brave brave brave bra
brave brave brave brave brave brave brave
ave brave brave brave brave brave brave bra
brave brave brave brave brave brave brave
ave brave brave brave brave brave brave bra
brave brave brave brave brave brave brave
ave brave brave brave brave brave brave bra
brave brave brave brave brave brave brave
ave brave brave brave brave brave brave bra
brave brave brave brave brave brave brave
ave brave brave brave brave brave brave bra
brave brave brave brave brave brave brave
ave brave brave brave brave brave brave bra

To _____

From _____

Date _____

100 DAYS
to brave

Devotions for Unlocking Your
Most Courageous Self

ANNIE F. DOWNS

ZONDERVAN

100 Days to Brave
Copyright © 2017 by Annie F. Downs

Requests for information should be addressed to:
Zondervan, 3900 Sparks Dr. SE, Grand Rapids, Michigan 49546

ISBN 978-0-310-08962-9

The author is represented by Alive Literary Agency, 7680 Goddard Street, Suite 200, Colorado Springs, Colorado 80920, www.aliveliterary.com.

Art direction: Adam Hill

Interior design: James Phinney

Printed in China

18 19 20 21   TIMS   10 9

Contents

>>>>—

Introduction

*D*ear friend,

This says a lot to me, you being here. It says you are feeling what I sometimes feel—like there is more than this. Your "this" may look different from my "this," but it's true all the same.

So I'm really glad you're here. And I hope you'll stick around all the way to the end because there is something here for you. At the least, it's an invitation to run after a life that might require a bit more courage but will certainly offer more joy and more than "this." At the most, everything changes. And that can be pretty awesome.

I hope you have a journal, or will buy a journal, to take alongside you in this daily story you are writing about your life. These 100 days are special to me, and I hope they will be to you as well. I've pulled together some of my favorite thoughts on courage and bravery and mixed them with lots of new ones that God and life and people have taught me over the last few years. And I think together with whatever God is already doing in your life, this could be a really interesting journey for you.

I know I'm not really there beside you, but in my heart it feels like I am. Think of me as the friend who's across the table from you at the local coffeehouse, just here to talk and process and think with you as you walk this road toward your most courageous self. I'm cheering for you.

Sincerely,

BRAVE ENOUGH
TO START

*You were always
meant to be brave.*

Day One

>>>> ———

WHAT IS BRAVE?

"For I am the LORD your God who takes hold of your right
hand and says to you, Do not fear; I will help you."

—ISAIAH 41:13 NIV

Brave. What is it? Truth is, there is no formula and there are
no rules. There is the Bible, our guidebook for all things, but
other than that, being brave is organic and spiritual and a
unique journey for each person.

I won't be saying, "Here is exactly what courage looks like" or
"If you want to really risk in a way that impacts the people around
you, do these particular things." I don't think that works. I don't
think you need me to tell you what to do. I think you know. (Or if
you don't, you will.) I think you just need a little pregame warm-up.
A little something to oomph you along. An understanding of the
map you are holding.

For the next 100 days, I want to show you that you are braver
than you know, and with that knowledge in your back pocket, you
can change your world.

Courage is doing things even when you're scared. Being brave isn't something that happens when you're not scared anymore. Brave people don't stop hearing the whispers of fear.

They hear the whispers but take action anyway.

Being brave is hearing that voice of fear in your head, but saying, "Okay, but the truth is, God made me on purpose and for a purpose."

I can tell you that the moments of my greatest fears—those times when I was sure I was going to wimp out under the pressure of it all—have also been the open doors to the greatest changes in my life. So I step out, full of fear, but trusting that God is on the other side in new and wonderful ways. And so far? He always is.

Brave people don't stop hearing the whispers of fear. They hear the whispers but take action anyway.

He will be for you too.

Be Brave: *Tell one person (a friend, a spouse, a coworker, a mentor) that you have begun this 100-day journey toward a braver life.*

Day Two

WHY BE BRAVE?

We can only keep on going, after all, by the power of God, who first saved us and then called us to this holy work. We had nothing to do with it. It was all his idea, a gift prepared for us in Jesus long before we knew anything about it. But we know it now.

—2 TIMOTHY 1:8–9 MSG

I got to travel to Honolulu, Hawaii, to speak at a conference. One afternoon I walked into the Kailua Starbucks to write for a bit and saw zero tables available. I didn't really have a plan B for where to write, so I got in line for my drink anyway.

A table opened up between a vacationing couple and three tan and adorable surfer dudes. The surfers were talking about their marriages, so I tuned out because, ya know, they had wives already.

I began to unpack, and just because of proximity (the tables were close, y'all), I couldn't help but check back into their conversation—and I heard them talking about absolute truth and how God is the only thing that is absolute, and suddenly I realized I was watching two of them share their stories of Jesus with the third.

My heart began to race. That conversation takes courage. Sharing your story takes guts.

I know. Maybe you think I'm being dramatic, but listen. That guy? Hearing how Jesus is the answer? His life is forever different and his future is forever altered because those two surfers were brave enough to say the things about Jesus that they know to be true.

Seeing other people be brave makes me want to be brave too. It's a domino effect.

I felt it in me as I listened to them—the want to share my story. That's why you'll see rational adults going down a loopty-loop waterslide even if they don't want to—because they want to show their kids it isn't scary.

Seeing other people be brave makes me want to be brave too.

That's why we have to start. That's why we have to go first. That's why we have to be brave—so that others will be inspired to be brave along with us.

We can be brave because we were always meant to be brave.

It is scary to be who you're meant to be. It doesn't feel easy because it's not. But we were made for this. Like today's scripture says, we have holy work. Why be brave? Because when we're brave enough to share the God stories in our lives, it changes the people around us. It changes us to share them.

BE BRAVE: *Think back on your day. Where can you see God working on your behalf? Or just showing up for you? Tell somebody.*

Day Three

YOU ARE BRAVER
THAN YOU KNOW

Whether you turn to the right or to the left, your ears will
hear a voice behind you, saying, "This is the way; walk in it."

—ISAIAH 30:21 NIV

In October 2007, I started to feel something unsettled in my spirit. That's the best way I can describe it. After weeks of this weird feeling, I felt like I had to really pray and ask God to direct me. I sensed I was supposed to make a change, but I just didn't know what that change was.

So I asked God. And my heart kept hearing that it was time for a move. To Nashville. And after a few months of wrestling, I did it.

I cried the entire drive. Three and a half hours. Now, I know I wasn't leaving for a town halfway around the world (yet), but this Georgia girl would be moving farther away from home than she ever dreamed.

Friend, you need to know this. I never *felt* brave. I never had a moment of extreme courage or belief that this was going to be the best decision I had ever made. I just did the next thing. Quit my job. Sold my house. Packed my belongings. Pointed north until I crossed the state line and didn't stop until I saw the trademark of the Nashville skyline—the Batman building.

I won't bore you with stories of the weeping and gnashing of teeth that occurred for the first weeks (okay, fine, months) after I moved, but it was terrible. Painful. Lonely.

Can I say this again? *I never felt brave.* But day after day, I just did the next thing, took the next step, said the next yes. And God built a life for me in Nashville that I could not have dreamed up for myself. I may not have felt brave, but I was taking brave steps in obedience to God.

> *I never felt brave. But day after day, I just did the next thing, took the next step, said the next yes.*

If you and I sat down and you told me your story, I would be able to show you places where you made brave choices, even if you don't label them that way. You're probably already doing more than you realize. You are braver than you know.

BE BRAVE: *Think back on your life. Journal about two or three moments you or someone else might label as "brave."*

Day Four

LOOK FOR BRAVE

The officials were amazed to see how brave Peter and John were, and they knew that these two apostles were only ordinary men and not well educated. The officials were certain that these men had been with Jesus.

—ACTS 4:13 CEV

Every day I hear story after story of courage. (Not a bad gig, to tell you the truth.)

You sweet people e-mail me, text me, and tag me on the Internet as you share your brave stories. And as I travel around the country and speak to groups, you cannot imagine how many stories of courage I get to hear.

Each time I think, *Man, I wish everyone could hear this!*

There is something superpowerful about putting brave on display—in your life, in the lives of the people you love, in the art you see or read or hear. When we see brave out in the world, it inspires us, doesn't it? I think that's why not only do we need to share our brave, but we need to actively look for it as well. I know you have friends, like I do, who are being braver than they knew they could be in their everyday lives.

Do you see brave when you look around your life? In the face in the mirror as well as in the faces you see when you are gathered with your people?

Who is displaying courage? Someone battling a disease? Acting in spite of fear? Chasing a dream?

Where do you see brave moments in your family? In your own life? In your friends?

When we see brave out in the world, it inspires us, doesn't it?

Are you reading something that sounds brave? Have you watched a film that reminded you of something brave? Courage is in the arts all the time. (And I'm not *just* referring to *Braveheart*, though I love Scotland and do find that movie inspiring in so many ways.) Sometimes I'll even look for movies or books along a theme that I am struggling with. Most recently, as a new relationship began to grow with a man in a different city, I read a book about a couple who survived a long-distance relationship. I needed their courage to remind me to be brave too. (Even though they were fictional and—spoiler alert—my relationship ended.)

I think when you hear other stories, they will sound like your story, and you will realize you are braver than you give yourself credit for. And we will cheer for each other and see courage in each other, and we will all be braver for it.

BE BRAVE: *When you see brave, say so.*

Day Five

JUST START

Saul said to David, "Go, and the LORD be with you."

—1 SAMUEL 17:37 NIV

think the hardest thing about writing is the blank page. Or computer screen. It's said that to be a writer is to have homework every day for the rest of your life. You remember that feeling, don't you? When you have a paper to write or an assignment to turn in and you know you can do it if you can just. Get. Started.

It's so hard to start, whether it's writing a book, training for a 5K, or any other dream you may have. To start the journey toward that thing—I don't know what it is for you—is not a journey *to* courage. The moment you take that first step, the moment you start, little seeds of courage, the ones I believe are already planted there right now, begin to sprout in your heart. You aren't headed out to find courage. It's in you, it is blooming, and it is with you as you travel and say yes to things that seem scary.

Those little seeds of courage have been growing in your heart for weeks, maybe years. Then at some point your heart began to beat with a different rhythm, and now here you are, ready to take the first brave step.

You just have to start, my friend. That thing that is whispering on your insides? Maybe for you it's writing a note. Singing a song. Making a phone call. Having a conversation.

> *The moment you take that first step, little seeds of courage begin to sprout in your heart.*

Composing a story. Writing a check. Booking that trip. Sending an e-mail. Going on a date. Reading a book. Signing up.

I'm trying to list as many options as possible, but you know the thing God is doing in your life better than I do. It's time to get quiet before the Lord and ask Him what it looks like for you to live a life of courage *today*.

Just start.

Be Brave: *What does it look like for you to take a step of courage today that will help you start?*

Brave Enough to Be You

The planet just really needs you to be you, okay?

Day Six

>>>———

THE LIES YOU BELIEVE

And the woman said to the serpent, "We may eat of the fruit of the trees in the garden, but God said, 'You shall not eat of the fruit of the tree that is in the midst of the garden, neither shall you touch it, lest you die.'" But the serpent said to the woman, "You will not surely die."

—Genesis 3:2–4 esv

*E*ve was the first woman deceived by words—but not the last. God had said one thing, Satan said another . . . and Eve fell for Satan's lies.

Sin and shame entered our world, and Jesus paid for it with His life. See, your struggle to separate truth from lies is something that every human wrestles with. It's hard to believe truth if your mind is flooded with confusion and false stories. And Satan is the one who is always trying to kill, steal, and destroy (John 10:10).

Satan is a liar. I know you know that, but I want to say it again: *he is a liar.* He wants to define you, label you, and stop you from being brave and doing the work God has for you.

When Satan lies to you (for instance, "You've got zero talent"), you begin to swirl that thought around in your head: *She's better at this job than I am. I'm definitely the dumbest person in this office.*

Soon, lies to yourself lead to lies about others ("Have you met the new office manager? Not very smart, that one . . .") because you are hurting and insecure.

You hear a lie, you treat it like truth, and it begins to define you, like a label. And then you act out of that label.

> *It's hard to believe truth if your mind is flooded with confusion and false stories.*

It's a vicious cycle that can be treated only by a heaping dose of truth—the real stuff. That's why I love the Bible. In His Word, God has already given you all the labels you need, and that's how we learn how to treat ourselves and each other.

Friend, it's time to stop listening to Satan's lies and labels so you can hear the truth.

Be Brave: *Read the story of David and Goliath (1 Samuel 17). What are some labels other people gave David? Which ones were actually true?*

Day Seven

THE TRUTH THAT SETS YOU FREE

Jesus answered, "It is written: 'Man shall not live on bread alone, but on every word that comes from the mouth of God.'"

—MATTHEW 4:4 NIV

There is so much to the story of Jesus' temptation in the wilderness—so many topics we could talk about—God's provision, the power of Scripture, temptation. But when we are thinking about being brave, this story is another example of truth versus lies and how believing truth produces courage.

Jesus was faced (like face-to-face) with temptation from Satan. The enemy. But Jesus stood up against the lies and spoke truth into the situation. Jesus knew the truth, and He *believed* it. Every time Satan offered something to Jesus, He responded with a scripture. Jesus repeatedly reminded Satan how this story really goes.

The truth that sets you free is God's Word. If you fill your mind with His words, that truth will make you brave. Page after page, verse after verse, God has already said who you are. You are released to believe that you are who He says you are. That the Bible is true. That you are deeply loved no matter what. Will you be brave enough to believe Him?

Believing truth is always a choice. In every situation, in every conversation, and in every moment that you begin to criticize yourself, you have the choice to fight for truth or give in to the lies.

There is so much power when you begin to understand that you are who God says you are, not who other people say you are or who you believe you are.

Let me tell you about believing in truth and how it changed my life. I'm free. I can live and speak and love openly because I believe *Believing truth is always a choice.* I am who God says I am. My insecurities are quieter (not gone, but quieter), my worries are lighter (not weightless, but lighter), and my heart is fuller because I know how God feels about me.

BE BRAVE: *Copy this prayer into your journal (or write one of your own):* God, tell me the truth of who I am. I'm listening. I want to be free from the lies—do that for me. Rescue me. Bring truth like a waterfall.

Day Eight

YOU AREN'T A MISTAKE

I praise you, for I am fearfully and wonderfully made.
Wonderful are your works; my soul knows it very well.

—PSALM 139:14 ESV

I like it when TV ads remind us to believe in ourselves and be confident we can do anything we want to do. You've seen the ones I'm talking about—an NBC star sits awkwardly on the arm of a couch and says into the camera, "You know those dreams you have? You can do them. Believe in yourself." And then the "ding ding ding ding" jingle plays as a star crosses the screen. The more you know, people. The more you know.

Here's something I know: I shouldn't believe in me, at least not in the way those commercials say I should. I've been me long enough to know that I am not someone to be believed in. I mess up. I hurt people's feelings. I care too much about some things and not enough about others.

I get lost. I am not perfect. And I don't want to pour my hope or trust into someone as faulty as me. So while I'm grateful for what the TV ads are saying, I don't think it is totally true.

I believe in the me God made and in the me God can make. I believe He made me on purpose and didn't make any mistakes when it came to my creation. That makes me feel brave.

And that is the place where I find my courage—knowing that while I am making mistakes, I am not a mistake. That is where you can find your courage too.

Maybe your parents never got married, maybe you were born without the ability to see or hear, or maybe you're missing a limb. Whatever it is, you aren't a mistake. God doesn't make mistakes.

While I am making mistakes, I am not a mistake.

I know my tendencies and fears, and I also know my gifts and hopes. It's where those meet that I often find God cheering for me to make the brave choice.

We can be confident in how God made us because His Word says we are fearfully and wonderfully made. But we can't do this life—or be brave—on our own.

Be Brave: *Remind someone you love—a friend, partner, child, spouse—that God doesn't make mistakes.*

Day Nine

YOUR HEART

But you, Lord, are a compassionate and gracious God, slow
to anger, abounding in love and faithfulness.

—PSALM 86:15 NIV

God loves to love you. I like to think that every time I take a breath, and every time my lungs pump blood into my heart, God has another loving thing to say about me. He's that good at it. Our God, the One who is breathing life into your life, is full of love for you—no matter what you have done or where you have been. For someone like me, who is pretty good at messing up and feeling guilty, it's really, really good to know that I can't make God love me any more or any less.

Consider the fact that in God's eyes, through Jesus, you are holy, chosen, dearly loved—*wow*. That quiets my fears—the ones that whisper I am alone, unlovable, unworthy—and makes me feel brave.

Allow God into your heart. Let Him into those little places inside that are hurt and alone and afraid. Let Him love you, lead you, and make you into the courageous person He has planned—because I promise that adventure will be the greatest of your life.

God loved me when I was totally and fully unlovable. In my deepest pit of sin, in the farthest corner of my rebellion, in the angriest moment of my hate, He chose to love me. And I've been known to be a total punk. Unfortunately, I will probably continue to be a punk at times. Yet He loves me to pieces—all my pieces. I cannot earn it, I don't deserve it, and yet I am drowning in it.

So I do the little bits that I can to love Him back—and you can do the same. What does that look like? Well, it looks like making brave, God-honoring life choices in response to His love.

Our God, the One who is breathing life into your life, is full of love for you—no matter what.

Has He given you a passion for something you haven't been brave enough to pursue? Do you love to sing? Sing a love song to God. Do you love to write? Write a book about your love for God. Do you love to dance? Draw? Play sports? Care for orphans or elderly people? Whatever it is, embrace the fact that you are loved and chosen by God, and take the courageous step of using these passions to love God back.

BE BRAVE: *How do you see your heart responding to God's love?*

Day Ten

YOUR FEET

Whoever says he abides in him ought to walk in the same
way in which he walked.

—1 John 2:6 esv

I sort of love my feet. Unlike my sausage fingers, my toes are pretty
well shaped. I love getting pedicures, and in fact, I've been pon-
dering what color I'd like to use, and I'm seriously considering a
bright-yellow polish color.

I've wanted it for a while, but my friends have peer-pressured
me away from it the last few times, encouraging other shades, like
various pinks. But I can't resist the urge for yellow anymore. And
I'm choosing to view it as a brave color choice, okay?

When I was a kid, I used to wear tennis shoes all the time. As
a soccer player and a tomboy, I always picked them. Tennis shoes
are a safe choice—they stay in place (unlike flip-flops, which can
flip here or flop there), they're comfortable (unlike most high heels),
and they last for quite a while. Actually, now that I'm thinking it
through, I still really love them.

Tennies allow us to do some amazing things with our feet, but one of the truest ways to glorify God with your feet is to lead. Lead people toward an abundant life and toward a real relationship with a real God. Lead people away from sin and choices that cause pain. Lead people with the way you live.

For many, leading anyone or anything is terrifying. For others, it feels natural— like the absolute best. But no matter how you're wired, using your feet to lead people takes bravery.

One of the truest ways to glorify God with your feet is to lead.

In the long run, you need to remember one thing: whether you're wearing bright-yellow toenail polish, helping out an elderly neighbor by mowing her grass, or washing the clothes of street kids in India, you were made to walk like Jesus walked. To serve. Because of God's great love for us, we can love and lead others. And we don't have to be afraid. We can be brave.

So take those feet and start walking and talking. Have courage and let your feet lead you down the path God has for you.

BE BRAVE: *What are some places where you are already leading? Thank God for them, and ask Him for even more opportunities.*

Day Eleven

>>>>———

YOUR MIND

Don't be like the people of this world, but let God change
the way you think. Then you will know how to do everything that is good and pleasing to him.

—Romans 12:2 cev

What's on your mind right now? Here are the thoughts that are
in my head this very minute (because I'm sure you're just on
the edge of your seat in anticipation): *Some guy I'm supposed
to know just came into the coffee shop. This chai latte is definitely
not the best I've ever had. Why isn't the Wi-Fi working? That guy has
a lot of beard hair. A lot.*

Everything in the body depends on the working of the mind.
The brain is the core organ. You can have a heart transplant, a leg or
an arm transplant, even a lung transplant. But there is no substitute
for the brain God has given you. Your mind is yours alone.

Our imaginations are amazing. Just think: every book, television show, movie, song, piece of furniture, street design, pair
of flip-flops—everything—was once an idea. Simply a thought in
someone's brain. And because your brain is so important—all of

your genius math equations, famous quotes, childhood songs, and fashion sense are housed there—it's vital that you protect it.

Your mind is a container, but it's a fragile container. So being brave means taking measures to protect it. Things are going to fill it—that's just the nature of your mind. It's up to you to decide what gets to fill that container.

What are the portals to your mind? Your eyes. Your ears. Those are the places you need to guard. What you hear and what you see will affect your brain (and heart) greatly. So having wisdom when it comes to intake matters so, so much.

Everything depends on the working of the mind.

At the same time, your mind can do many good things for you. Use it well—create beautiful things; follow through with great ideas; love people who pop into your mind. If God has put the sparks of an idea into your mind, you can be brave enough to follow through. (Trust the sparks, friend; trust the sparks.)

Our minds are so powerful. I'm praying that you would ask for God to give you His mind, the mind of Christ. And that you would be brave enough to protect your mind, allow God to change the way you think, and then change this world with the ideas that can become reality. (Those sparks. I believe in them!)

Be Brave: *What is one thought, one spark, one idea in your head that you think God may have put there? Write it down. (And at some point, do something with the spark!)*

Day Twelve

>>>>———

SPEAK KINDLY
TO YOURSELF

The tongue has the power of life and death, and those who
love it will eat its fruit.

—PROVERBS 18:21 NIV

This morning when I did not like the look of the jeans I put on,
I told myself so. Old Annie would have continued a barrage of
ugly remarks about my looks, but instead, I looked in the mirror
and said, "Hey, put on a different pair. No biggie." And I shook it off
and changed.

See how Proverbs 18:21 says everything you say is either pro-
ducing life or death? It's just as true when you talk to yourself as
when you are speaking to others. Just like with my jeans this morning, I have to choose words of life over words of death. That's the
kind of conversations I want to have with myself—the ones that are
truthful, kind, and full of life.

Friend, stop being mean to yourself. Seriously. If you are going
to be the person who does the brave things God is calling you to do,

speaking life and developing beautiful things in others with your words, it begins with doing that for yourself.

Self-talk is a big part of everyone's life. We constantly and subconsciously have thoughts running through our minds that direct our days. You need to listen to those. The negative ones? The ones that cut you down and make you feel unloved and afraid? Time to chuck them. Stop yourself, identify the lie, and say the truth in its place.

Speaking kindly to yourself will make you brave.

Speaking kindly to yourself will make you brave. And if you're having trouble finding reasons to speak kindly to yourself, remember: It's not that you have earned the love of God or that you deserve love. God loves us, even though we don't deserve it (1 John 4:19).

You haven't earned this love; it's a gift. We don't attempt to beat the lies and believe the truth and love ourselves because we are perfect. We do it because in our imperfections, God loves us deeply and has made us just the way He wanted.

You can speak kindly to yourself because God loves you deeply because you are His. Speak kindly to yourself, as Jesus speaks kindly to you. Those words have power, and if you believe them, you will be brave.

BE BRAVE: *Write yourself a quick note and list three things you are thankful for about yourself. (Seriously. Do it.)*

Day Thirteen

LIKE WHAT YOU LIKE

For the Spirit God gave us does not make us timid, but gives us power, love and self-discipline.

—2 Timothy 1:7 niv

G rowing up, I wish I knew that I could like anything I wanted to like.

I loved playing in the middle school band. I've always been a huge music fan. In fact, I taught myself to play the piano by using a tiny three-octave electric keyboard and a hymnal that my choir director gave us at the end of third grade.

So when I entered middle school, I immediately joined the band. It was a tough choice between band and orchestra because I couldn't decide between the French horn and the cello. While my friend and neighbor Grace joined the orchestra, I felt the pull to the French horn. And boy, did I love that thing.

When it was time to go to high school, though, I quit because I thought it was uncool to be in the band. My self-esteem was so low that I gave up something I really enjoyed because I was working so hard to be perceived as cool.

If I had been brave enough to pursue what I liked back then, I would have kept playing the French horn and probably would have really enjoyed it. Maybe I'd be performing in the Nashville Symphony now instead of wondering if I even remember how to play the instrument. But I thought it was more important to do the "cool thing" than to do the thing I loved. I needed everyone else's approval since I didn't have my own.

I thought it was more important to do the "cool thing" than to do the thing I loved. I needed everyone else's approval since I didn't have my own.

I wish that was just a problem I had when I was a kid, but it's not. At times I still have to be confident in the person I want to be and what I want to do, even if it isn't cool or popular.

You know what's brave? Giving yourself permission to do the thing you want to do, to like whatever *you* want to like.

That's my hope for you. That as you grow to love yourself more and more, you will feel brave enough to love the things you love instead of altering them because you think that's what it will take to be accepted.

You are accepted by God. And hopefully you accept you too.

BE BRAVE: *I love making lists. So today make a list of five things that you really like: hobbies, musicians, food, places, TV shows. Give yourself permission to really like what you like.*

Day Fourteen

GOD MADE YOU ON PURPOSE

The LORD will fulfill his purpose for me; your steadfast love, O LORD, endures forever. Do not forsake the work of your hands.

—Psalm 138:8 ESV

I like the idea that God only made me once. Like paintings—there's something special about the first one. My cousin Joe just recently passed away, but for my entire life, he was a painter. An artist. My home is filled with paintings and sketches and illustrations he made just for me. In fact, one of the paintings he gave me proudly hangs in my dining room. It's huge and abstract and purple and blue and black and weird. I love it. A few years ago, I asked Joe what it's like to replicate art versus painting the original piece.

The short answer he gave is that the original is work, but fun. Any copies, exact or modified, are boring, if not mindless. Creating is just problem solving, and once you solve the original problem, it's like you could train bright monkeys to do the replicating. (That's a quote. "Bright monkeys." Man, I miss Joe.) The question is not unlike asking a chef to create the most special French onion soup in the world and, after he or she has succeeded beyond any expectations, to keep making it every day.

God made you once. You were worth the work that first time. Then He threw away that mold because one of you is enough for Him. You're enough. You are the sacred painting, the original.

God made us this way on purpose. It's no mistake that we are formed the way we are. But why? Why did God make humans in the first place?

Look at Isaiah 43:7: "Everyone who is called by *my* name, whom *I* created for *my* glory, whom *I* formed and made" (ESV, emphasis mine).

God created us for His glory. Hang with me for a little Old Testament lesson. The word *create* in the original Hebrew is *bara*. When this particular word is used, God is the only subject—He does all the work. Only He can create in this particular way. We may be able to create a painting or create chaos, but as humans, we cannot *bara*. So when God made you, He did something that only He can do, and He did that for His glory.

If we are each as unique as the Bible says we are, then our calls to courage are each equally unique.

This short Hebrew 101 lesson does have a point. We look at the original language of the text to see, according to Scripture, that we were made especially by God to promote Him, glorify Him, and worship Him.

So what does this have to do with being brave?

If we are each as unique as the Bible says we are, then our calls to courage are each equally unique.

We each have to be brave in our own ways. The painting of your life is a masterpiece that will never be replicated, and there's a brave brush to use in this painting that will change everything for God's glory and for your good. Maybe you want to move to another country to live and share about Jesus. My friend, that is brave. It really is. But so is being a stay-at-home mom. And so is being a cable technician. So is being an author or a baseball player or a chef. Courage looks different for each of us.

God made you on purpose and unique. God has called you to be brave. And God will equip you to do it.

Be Brave: *In your journal, or here in the margins, list some ways your life is unique. What do you love? How do you like to spend your time? What ways do you see your life as different from anyone else's?*

BRAVE ENOUGH
TO BELIEVE GOD

He is who He says
He is. I promise.

Day Fifteen

ASK THE HARD QUESTIONS

"Call to me and I will answer you and tell you great and unsearchable things you do not know."

—JEREMIAH 33:3 NIV

The fall in Scotland, my other home, is beautiful and crisp and the days get short in a blink, but those early-afternoon hours take on a golden hue that I've never seen before. After lunch one day in early October, I sat at the Starbucks across the street from the Eric Liddell Centre with just my journal, my Bible, a peach muffin, and a soy chai.

I felt totally alive. It was like every internal cylinder was firing and I was the optimum Annie. I began to journal, wondering what was causing my heart to live in a perpetual state of pure, happy explosion.

So I asked God a question: *What is it, God, that makes me feel so alive?*

At the time, that didn't seem like a hard question, but sometimes just opening the lines of communication with God allows the Holy Spirit to lead you to the harder places.

I made a list of all the things that were true of my life at the moment. I was living in Scotland, I was single, and I was doing college ministry.

And quietly in my heart, I heard God say, *You can do college ministry anywhere.*

And I knew. I sat back in my chair, a little in awe, and said out loud to no one and everyone, "Oh. I'm going home." Back to Nashville.

Sometimes we avoid asking God things because we fear what the answer will be, whether we're asking Him why our lives feel so good, why He placed us where we are now, where He wants us to go next, or why something painful in our lives is still so painful. However, when it is God who answers, it isn't something to be scared of.

Sometimes we avoid asking God things because we fear what the answer will be.

It takes bravery to ask the hard questions and listen for hard answers. But knowing that God works for your good and that His answers can be trusted is a great remedy for fear.

Don't be afraid to ask God the things you really want to know. You may not get the answer you expect, but you will get an answer. Maybe sometimes you won't know why. Or you don't really want to know why. Or you don't even know what you're asking or what His answer will lead you to or away from.

Whatever it is, you can ask. Even if and when things are hard, you can always ask God, *What's Your plan for me? What am I supposed to be learning right now?* And He will show You the answer. And those answers, my friend? They are the answers that bring peace. Ask God the hard questions.

Be Brave: *What is one question you've been afraid to bring to God? Ask Him the question right now, out loud, and listen for His answer.*

Day Sixteen

BELIEVE YOU ARE NEVER ALONE

"And surely I am with you always, to the very end of the age."

—MATTHEW 28:20 NIV

When God made it clear that He wanted me to move to Nashville, I was terrified. I barely like to go to the bathroom alone—I certainly didn't want to move to a new *state* alone. To live in a place other than Georgia felt absolutely foreign.

On New Year's Day, I told two of my best friends, Haley and Molly. We sat on Haley's living room floor as I shared the story, and thankfully they were on my side—the side that said moving was a lunatic idea and I had for sure made it up. "If you want to be a writer," Haley said, "can't you just do that in Atlanta? There have got to be a lot of Atlanta writers around." For a solid twenty minutes, we brainstormed. Then we stopped, and tears leaked down our faces as we realized the truth. God was asking me to be braver than I had ever thought possible, and it was going to bring sadness to us all. I was about to willingly walk into a season when I would feel very alone.

Then August came along, and all of a sudden, it was done. The thing that had been in the front of my mind and prayers and worries was no longer off in the future. It was here. I was here.

No friends. No church. No family. No idea where to find the post office, grocery store, or hospital. Alone.

Or at least, I *felt* alone. But I wasn't. Do you know what *Immanuel* means? It is one of God's names and means "God with us." Because Jesus paid the price for our sin, God is always with us. Jesus said He would be with us until the end of time.

Even when you feel alone, you actually aren't.

See? Even when you feel alone, you actually aren't. He is the One who sticks with you no matter what.

And you are brave enough to believe that what He said is true. He is always with you. Believe it. Do the hard thing God is leading you to do. You are never alone.

BE BRAVE: *Just look in the mirror today and say to yourself, "Friend, you are never alone." (I do this a lot—such a good reminder.)*

Day Seventeen

DIG INTO THE WORD
FOR YOURSELF

Every part of Scripture is God-breathed and useful one way or another—showing us truth, exposing our rebellion, correcting our mistakes, training us to live God's way. Through the Word we are put together and shaped up for the tasks God has for us.

—2 TIMOTHY 3:16–17 MSG

I became a Christian when I was five, so the Bible has always been a part of my reading life. I am thankful that as long as I have known how to read, I have had a Bible. But I haven't always enjoyed reading it. To be honest, parts of it can bore me—lists, laws, and things that my brain doesn't quite understand.

But as the years have gone by, I have grown to see the Bible for what it really is—a collection of stories with people just like us, life lessons, and page after page describing the God we love and serve.

If you set out to read your Bible as if it is something you *have* to do, you will miss out on the supernatural power it can have in your life. The Bible is God's way of communicating with you, of letting you in on who He is. The Holy Spirit uses His Word to show us the truth, convict us, correct us, and train us.

The Bible isn't boring. It isn't just lists, or just rules, or just a bunch of stories that are hard to understand. It's a record of who God is and the story of His great love for His people—and that's us.

The more you dig into the Word for yourself, the more you will hunger for it. The more you read the Bible, the more you will know God.

The Bible is always your best resource when you want to hear from God. There, in black and white (and sometimes red), are God-inspired words for you. Don't rely on your pastor, a podcast, or even a Christian author to read a few verses here and there. Dig into the Word for yourself, and enjoy this gift God has given you—total access to who He is and total knowledge of how He feels about you!

If you set out to read your Bible as if it is something you have to do, you will miss out on the supernatural power it can have in your life.

BE BRAVE: *Check out SheReadsTruth.com (or HeReadsTruth.com). They offer lots of plans and resources to help you learn to read the Bible on a regular basis.*

Day Eighteen

PRAY

This is the confidence we have in approaching God: that if
we ask anything according to his will, he hears us.

—1 JOHN 5:14 NIV

've had a long (and maybe complicated) relationship with prayer.
I know it is real; I know it is powerful; I know God hears us.
However, that doesn't mean I have always gotten what I wanted.
But the first time I remember God absolutely answering one of my
prayers was when I was nine years old. In the spring of my third-
grade year, I starred in our church's children's musical. Okay, to say
I was "THE STAR" is a bit of an exaggeration because, while it was
true in my heart, I'm pretty sure I was just one of the stars. Fine, one
of the cast members.

I was Little Psalty. (For those who don't know, Psalty is a singing
hymnal who teaches children about God.) I strapped on this huge
blue cardboard costume shaped like a hymnal and threw a baseball
bat over my shoulder. I then walked through the crowd, singing the
beautiful old hymn "Take My Life and Let It Be."

Oh, did I mention I was a male character? So that's a special part of the story.

When I got home from school the day of the musical, my mom was in her bed, all the lights off in her room, with a migraine. My life is filled with memories of migraines. When I was a kid, we took my mother to the hospital for them or left the house with my dad so she would have peace and quiet. That day when I saw my mom in bed, I knew immediately that it was bad.

She whispered to me in her headache voice that she was sorry, but she wasn't going to be able to make it to the performance that night.

Well, my tender little third-grade heart was broken. I ran up the stairs to my room, threw my book bag on the floor, knelt down beside my bed, clasped my hands together, and prayed as hard as my heart knew how to pray.

Prayer is this amazing opportunity to connect directly with the greatest Being who has always been.

I don't recall every word spoken during that fervent-kid prayer; I know I prayed God would heal Mama's headache so she could come to the performance. I begged like only a nine-year-old knows how, with eyes squeezed tight and repeating the same few phrases over and over again.

Later that night at the church, with just minutes until the curtain went up, someone whispered my name. I was standing on the risers, ready to sing, and there was my mom, on the side of the stage, telling me she had made it.

I know. It's like a Hallmark movie moment. And that's when I learned that prayer is powerful.

Since then, I've had prayers answered just like that, in the exact way I thought, and I've had prayers seemingly never answered. I've had other situations I prayed about that went so differently that I wondered if God and I spoke the same language.

I think that's where the courage comes in. Are you brave enough to pray and believe that God hears you and changes things? Are you brave enough to believe with your whole heart that God will do something miraculous? Are you brave enough to say the first words to Him after you've been silent for a while? Prayer isn't about us, really. Prayer is this amazing opportunity to connect directly with the greatest Being who has always been. And it takes courage to know that for yourself.

So pray. God is absolutely real. And He is listening.

BE BRAVE: *Pray today, whether it is a short sentence muttered under your breath or a few paragraphs written out in your journal. Talk to God. He is listening.*

Day Nineteen

>>>>———>

HAVE FAITH

Now faith is confidence in what we hope for and assurance
about what we do not see.

—HEBREWS 11:1 NIV

What does it mean to actually believe God? What is faith?
Faith is being sure. And convinced.

Sometimes it's hard to feel sure. So what do you do if
you want to have faith or you want more faith and you're not sure
how to get it? Ask God to fill you with faith—faith in Him, faith in
His promises, faith in His ways. And then use the assurance welling
up in your heart to fight off the lies of the enemy.

The enemy is so good at lying, isn't he? (You know you have
an enemy, right? A legit enemy who has no good thoughts toward
you or for you.) He's been lying since the garden of Eden when he
convinced Eve that God wasn't really true or trustworthy. And that's
the same lie he whispers to us. Lies like, "You can't trust God . . .
Your faith is weak . . . Do you even *have* faith?"

When Satan pushes your buttons or makes you doubt God's
Word or God's love for you, what's your first brave move? Hold

up the shield of faith that you hold over your heart, meant to protect you from the arrows of the enemy. Just believe. It isn't always easy—in fact it rarely is, but the good stuff is never cheap. And what happens to your soul on the other side of a fight for faith is the good stuff.

Ask God to fill you with faith— faith in Him, faith in His promises, faith in His ways.

Your next brave move? Fix your eyes on Jesus, who is the "pioneer and perfecter" of your faith (Hebrews 12:2 NIV). When doubts cloud your mind and faith doesn't come easily, remember that He considered it a joy to endure the cross because of His great love for you. And He will help you grow in faith.

Be sure of this: when you ask God to increase your faith, He will.

BE BRAVE: *Download Matt Wertz's song "Keep Faith" and put it on repeat for a bit today. Maybe journal some of the lyrics that stick out to you.*

Day Twenty

GOD IS WHO HE SAYS HE IS

God is not human, that he should lie, not a human being, that he should change his mind. Does he speak and then not act? Does he promise and not fulfill?

—NUMBERS 23:19 NIV

You know who had some serious courage? Gideon. The one from the Bible.

In Judges 6, all the Israelites were misbehaving in serious ways—the kind of ways that separate them from God. The Lord gave them over to their enemies, and they were living in fear—hiding away and being defeated and robbed. Then the Israelites began to cry out to God for rescue. (I know that move, don't you? Hiding from God when I feel like I've messed up but then asking Him to rescue me when I've gotten myself in a bad spot.) God decided to show mercy and deliver them, defeating the other armies by using the Israelite army. And Gideon, this unlikely little guy, was about to have a unique call to courage.

Starting in Judges 6:11, we see Gideon threshing his wheat while hiding out in a winepress (instead of separating the wheat in a normal public place). An angel of the Lord appeared and said, "The LORD is with you, mighty warrior" (Judges 6:12 NIV). This statement surprised Gideon because, well, he was *hiding*, which is not your typical "mighty warrior" behavior. But the Lord told Gideon that he was the guy who would lead the army to save Israel from the Midianites.

When he heard this, Gideon immediately started explaining to God why he was the wrong guy for the job—he belonged to the weakest clan, and he was the weakest of the weakest clan. You know what was happening there? Gideon was looking at himself and his own abilities rather than looking at God and believing that He is who He says He is.

You are deeply loved and called to be courageous by a God who is perfect and perfectly trustworthy.

You are deeply loved and called to be courageous by a God who is perfect and perfectly trustworthy.

If you feel stuck looking at your own shortcomings, look upward to your Jesus, who is exactly who He says He is, who defeated death itself, and who empowers you to be brave.

BE BRAVE: *Are you hiding from God right now? You don't have to hide! God is making you brave day by day.*

Day Twenty-One

YOU CAN HEAR GOD

"The shepherd walks right up to the gate. The gatekeeper opens the gate to him and the sheep recognize his voice. He calls his own sheep by name and leads them out. When he gets them all out, he leads them and they follow because they are familiar with his voice."

—JOHN 10:2–4 MSG

I had always lived in Georgia. For the first twenty-seven years of my life, I had called one state home. I liked my Georgia driver's license, my Georgia sports teams, my Georgia sticker on my car, and my Georgia home.

Then one October I felt something stirring in my heart about Nashville, Tennessee. I was scared. I didn't want to even think about moving, much less really do it. But I've been following God a long time, and I have learned to hear God's voice in my life. I knew that quiet voice and that gentle push.

I didn't want to go. I can remember my last church service in Georgia before my big move. As the music played, tears puddled in my eyes and lots of things ran through my mind: This was my last Sunday at home, everything was about to change, maybe God would change His mind, maybe I was wrong all along . . . Wait. Maybe God would change His mind?

I'm a genius, I thought. *I'll just pray and ask Him to change His mind. He knows I am* willing *to go—I've already paid my first month's rent and I moved one carload of stuff to Nashville. Now He'll let me out of it.*

So that's exactly what I prayed. While the rest of the people worshipped God, I bartered with Him. I reminded Him how totally *willing*

I've been following God a long time, and I have learned to hear God's voice in my life.

I was to go. I knew sometimes He doesn't actually make you *do* the thing, just be willing to. I begged Him not to make me go. I begged Him to change His mind.

And then a quietly bold statement ran through my mind and plugged right into my heart.

Nashville is the greatest gift I have ever given you.

I took a deep breath. I knew it was true. It didn't feel true. It didn't look true. But I knew that was God, and I knew it was truth.

It didn't feel like a gift for a long time. It felt terrible at first, then okay, then survivable, then good, then great. But I'll tell you what: that one sentence that God whispered into my heart years ago is one of the truest things I know today.

Nashville is the greatest gift God has ever given me. For sure. No question. He knew it then. We both know it now.

I strongly disagree with the people who say God doesn't speak to us anymore. I think He is always speaking to us—through the Bible, through nature, through others, through Jesus' life, and directly through the Holy Spirit who lives in us. You can hear Him too, if you want to. He's speaking, and He will talk to you if you're listening.

Be Brave: *Could you be brave enough today to believe that God wants to speak to you? Just ask Him. Pray this:* God, I want to hear You. I want to know Your voice and recognize it. I'm listening. Speak to me.

Day Twenty-Two

>>>> ————→

YOU ARE WHO GOD
SAYS YOU ARE

Therefore, as God's chosen people, holy and dearly loved,
clothe yourselves with compassion, kindness, humility,
gentleness and patience.

—Colossians 3:12 niv

My friend Jenna got a job at a bank in Nashville. She was so
excited during her training when her trainer told her she
would be learning how to identify counterfeit money. In her
sassy business suit, Jenna went to work that day expecting to see
and feel every different kind of counterfeit currency the FBI knew
about. She loves that kind of stuff—like those shows on television
dedicated to busting people breaking the law.

So when Jenna arrived that morning, she had a definite bounce
in her step, ready to start on the next undercover show. Instead, the
trainers handed her and her fellow new employees stacks of real
money and asked each person to count a stack. Over and over. And
then again. And over again. I don't know if this is totally accurate,

but Jenna swears she counted the fifty one-dollar bills more than one hundred times.

Frustrated, one of the other new workers asked their trainer, "Why are we doing this?"

The trainer responded, "Now you know how real money feels. You have practiced so much with the real thing that you will easily notice the fakes."

When you spend time with God and immerse yourself in the truth of His Word, you will easily notice the lies and the things you hear in your head that aren't really you.

When you spend time with God and immerse yourself in the truth of His Word, you will easily notice the lies and the things you hear in your head that aren't really you. You will hear the truth of who God says you are much more clearly, like how you are dearly loved.

All over His Word, you will find that God says: You are accepted. You are a friend of God. His heir. You are completely forgiven!

You are secure. Romans 8 says that you are free from condemnation. You are significant! Ephesians 2 says that you are God's workmanship, seated with Jesus in the heavenly realms.

All over His Word, God says that you are strong and important on this planet. You are who God says you are, and you can be brave.

BE BRAVE: *Finish this sentence: I am significant because _____ _____, and here are three ways that impacts my life: _____.*

Day Twenty-Three

>>>>

BELIEVE GOD CARES ABOUT YOUR DREAMS

"If you, then, though you are evil, know how to give good gifts to your children, how much more will your Father in heaven give good gifts to those who ask him!"

—MATTHEW 7:11 NIV

What does it look like to dream and believe that God is working in those dreams, even if they don't turn out? Do you trust that God wants to use those dreams?

I am living a life I never planned. And it has required more courage than I ever thought could fit in this five-foot-six-inch frame. Honestly, I am shocked that I am in my mid-thirties and have no husband and no children. But deep down in me is a fireball of hope. Not necessarily hope in the "I am *for sure* getting married someday" way, but hope in the "God knows what He is doing" kind of way.

I thought it would be way cooler to write about this later in my life. Like, when I am married to some awesome dude and we have three kids and a nice kitchen and I drive a cool-mom SUV and tiny shoes are scattered all throughout our house. Then I could tell all the singles to "hang in there because God has an amazing plan for your life!" And the section on singleness would be full of exclamation points because I find exclamation points to be very! encouraging! and uplifting!

But I am not going to stop hoping and dreaming. I think there is something really powerful about being smack in the middle of the unwanted season and being able to look you right in the eyeball (which I would if I could) and say, "God has not forgotten you. Your life and your dreams are important to God."

I just want to tell you, from one in the trenches of this season of wanting something I don't have (like most of us, I bet), that I am going to make it just fine. And if you are single and want to be married, or wishing you could have kids, or wanting a better job or home or city, I want you to know that you are going to make it too.

God has not forgotten you.

God hears us when we pray. He knows our hearts better than we do. He cares about you, and He cares about your dreams. So share your dreams with your Father, who loves you and loves to give you good gifts.

BE BRAVE: *What dream is in your heart that you haven't seen God do for you yet? What would it look like to be full of hope, even if you don't know how this story is going to end?*

Brave Enough to Dream

It's the brave ones who choose to dream.

Day Twenty-Four

DREAM BIG

And while [Jesus] was at Bethany in the house of Simon the leper, as he was reclining at table, a woman came with an alabaster flask of ointment of pure nard, very costly, and she broke the flask and poured it over his head. There were some who said to themselves indignantly, "Why was the ointment wasted like that? For this ointment could have been sold for more than three hundred denarii and given to the poor." And they scolded her. But Jesus said, "Leave her alone. Why do you trouble her? She has done a beautiful thing to me."

—MARK 14:3–6 ESV

Ever since third grade, my big dream was to teach school. I'm bossy by nature. Being a teacher is a great outlet for bossy people like me.

Midway through my senior year at the University of Georgia, right before I began my student-teaching experience, my campus pastor at the Wesley Foundation, Bob Beckwith, came to me with an opportunity. Wesley allows students to stay on after their senior year as unpaid interns, and Bob wanted me to be the women's ministry intern.

My big dream of teaching was in view, and all I had to do was fill out the right county applications and try to find a teaching job.

On the other hand, interning sounded awesome. Many of my good friends were interning, including my best friend and roommate, and I had grown so much within that ministry that the opportunity to serve in return felt right too.

But it was unpaid, and to intern at Wesley I had to raise $15,000. *Fifteen thousand dollars.*

On a Saturday morning before Christmas break, I sat in a comfy chair and read Mark 14:3–6. The woman with a flask of ointment gave everything she had to Jesus. Her heart, her sacrifice, and one year's wages.

God's dream for me was so much greater than the one I'd been planning all along.

I knew I was being asked to push pause on my big dream—to give up a year's wages as an offering to Jesus to serve college students and to minister to Jesus Himself—what I now see as God's biggest dream for my life.

I did end up being a schoolteacher for five years after that. It still amazes me how God's dream for me was so much greater than the one I'd been planning all along.

Dream big. Be brave enough to believe that as much as you could want, God could give to you. We are meant to make a big impact on the planet. Bigger than we could ever dream up on our own.

Be Brave: *List one or two really big dreams you have for your life.*

Day Twenty-Five

DREAM IN PIECES

The LORD who rescued me from the paw of the lion and the paw of the bear will rescue me from the hand of this Philistine.

—1 SAMUEL 17:37 NIV

God knows me. He knows you. He knows we need dreams in pieces because we would be too scared of the whole puzzle. Had I known I'd be an author and a speaker back when I was in college studying to be an elementary school teacher, I probably would have crawled under my covers and stayed there for a year or five. I'm here today because of the little steps and the brave moments dotted throughout my writing career that have grown into this.

He knows we need dreams in pieces because we would be too scared of the whole puzzle.

I think of King David, way back when he was a kid checking on his brothers in the battle against the Philistines. He found that everyone was scared of Goliath, this beast of a man who was fighting for the other army.

Young David the shepherd told King Saul he would go against Goliath. Everyone was stunned because David was a kid, and the rest of the Israelite army—adult men—were afraid of him. David's response shows us the importance of those daily steps of courage that lead to the bigger story.

> But David said to Saul, "Your servant has been keeping his father's sheep. When a lion or a bear came and carried off a sheep from the flock, I went after it, struck it and rescued the sheep from its mouth. When it turned on me, I seized it by its hair, struck it and killed it. Your servant has killed both the lion and the bear; this uncircumcised Philistine will be like one of them, because he has defied the armies of the living God." (1 Samuel 17:34–36 NIV)

David, as a shepherd boy, fought a lion. And a bear. And rescued his sheep. He never killed the lion in preparation for the bear. He didn't kill the bear in preparation for Goliath. He just chose to be brave at every turn—to do his job and protect the sheep. And as the challenges grew in scope, so did David's belief in the ways God had uniquely created him. More importantly, David wholly believed in who God is and that God had a role for him to play that would require courage. The same is true for me and you.

BE BRAVE: *What's one area of your life where you know you are being brave right now?*

Day Twenty-Six

>>>———————→

WHAT'S AN OPEN DOOR?

He leads me in paths of righteousness for his name's sake.

—PSALM 23:3 ESV

How do you know when to make a brave move, even if it isn't easy? How do you know when to just go for it?

As a sophomore in college (and for most of my college career), I loved spending time in the offices of my campus ministry, the University of Georgia Wesley Foundation—it felt cool and trendy and Christian.

A campus ministry is a church for college students set on a college campus. Many of my youth group friends also attended UGA, so every time I stopped by the Wesley building felt like a homecoming of sorts. And when I walked through the halls, I saw the photos of mission trips from past years.

One day I stood in front of one of those pictures—a group of college students clumped together in a sunflower field. The sun was shining on their heads, almost making the curly blonde girl look like she was glowing. Across the bottom it read, "SCOTLAND."

I had heard of Scotland. That was about it. During a Wednesday night service at Wesley that fall—just weeks later, really—the mission trips were announced for that school year, and I saw Scotland as an option. *Yeah*, I thought, *I want to stand in that field and take that sunflower picture.*

It wasn't superspiritual. It was an open door.

I knew the Bible said to go into all the nations and share the gospel (Matthew 28:19), so it was more about picking from the list of trips that would be offered for the interested students that semester. I prayed; I remember that. But there was no huge Scotland banner flying outside my bedroom window or any other weird signal from the heavens on this one. I just knew I wanted to go on a mission trip, and that was the one that stood out to me.

I ended up going on that mission trip, and even wound up living there for a time. Going on a trip overseas, and later to live there, took courage. It was different. It was new. And I wasn't following a path lit with bright arrows. It was an open door that God led me through.

It wasn't superspiritual. It was an open door.

In today's passage, the psalmist said that God led him down the path of righteousness. Ask the Lord to lead *you* to the open doors, then be brave enough to walk through them.

BE BRAVE: *Write out a prayer to God, asking Him to show you the open doors in your life right now. If you want Him to open the right doors and close the wrong ones, write that as well.*

Day Twenty-Seven

>>>> ──────→

WHAT'S A CLOSED DOOR?

Commit to the LORD whatever you do, and he will establish your plans.

—PROVERBS 16:3 NIV

Brave people charge through doors, right? Brave people see that a door isn't open and then they get creative and charge through and find another way, right?

Well, that's definitely how it goes *sometimes*, but as people who are reliant on an all-knowing God, we know that we can be doing our thing, walking, praying that we are in alignment with God's will, and we'll come to a closed door.

Closed doors can be confusing.

Maybe you were seeking God about what career path you should choose. Maybe you started preparing to be a marine biologist all the way back in high school with a summer job at the aquarium.

Maybe you lived in Florida. Your aunt was a marine biologist. Everything about this dream of yours made sense.

But then life happened. And you found yourself two years into college, looking at open doors you didn't expect, and realizing that the door to marine biology didn't seem to be something you could do anymore for some reason—not getting into a program, being short on finances, dealing with a family crisis that caused you to have to take a year off from school.

> *Sometimes we can be doing our thing, walking, praying that we are in alignment with God's will, and we'll come to a closed door.*

Whatever it is, it happens, and when it happens, you can be brave.

You can be brave because you can trust God. Brave people commit their work to the Lord and trust that His plan for their lives might not look the way they planned. And that's okay.

If you're looking at a closed door today, then there's an open one just around the corner. Be brave enough to walk through the doors that the Lord leads you through. Even when they are unexpected or feel scary.

BE BRAVE: *This may be a bit painful or scary, but write about a door you know God has closed in your life.*

Day Twenty-Eight

>>>>———

MOURN DREAMS
THAT HAVE DIED

My soul melts away for sorrow; strengthen me according
to your word!

—PSALM 119:28 ESV

I wanted to live in Scotland for eleven years before I ever did it.
Eleven years. Multiple times during my twenties, I had opportunities to move there, and I always said no. The timing wasn't
ever quite right, I never felt like it was God's best plan, but also, in
the back of my head . . . *I was scared.* I was scared that moving to
Scotland would mean I would never get married.

I always dreamed I'd be married with kids before I reached my
thirties, and because of that dream, I let an entire decade go by in
hopes that choosing America meant choosing marriage. Now, I'm
not saying that staying in America was out of God's will. I know He
did good things with my life in that decade; I just know that each
time one of those opportunities was placed before me, fear whispered to me. And I listened.

I sat with my counselor two weeks ago, and as counseling appointments tend to go, I verbally vomited everything I had been processing during the weeks since our last meeting. When I was done, she looked me straight in the eyes and told me it was okay to mourn.

"Wait," I said. "I don't think I agree with that. I think I'm supposed to be fine that this is God's plan and that I trust Him and that He is working all things—"

She interrupted me.

"The dreams you thought would come true in a certain time frame never did. You saw a life for yourself that you will never have. You can mourn that loss."

"The dreams you thought would come true in a certain time frame never did. You saw a life for yourself that you will never have. You can mourn that loss."

No one had ever said that to me before. But I needed to hear it. I may not have gotten married in the decade I planned, but God led me down amazing paths where I was able to glorify Him.

It's easy to take the unanswered prayers and disappointments in our lives and brush them under the rug so we don't have to think about them. But you know what, friend? It's okay to mourn your dreams that have died. Looking at those dreams takes bravery. But when you look them in the face, head-on, and let them go, you will see how God's plan for your life, although different from what you expected, is a beautiful story of its own that you never could have dreamed up for yourself.

BE BRAVE: *What dead dream do you need to mourn?*

Day Twenty-Nine

>>>>

CHASE THE DREAMS THAT ARE ALIVE

The purposes of a person's heart are deep waters, but one who has insight draws them out.

—Proverbs 20:5 niv

Sometimes being brave is walking away from the dreams that have died and the doors that have closed and chasing the dreams that are alive.

God plants dreams in our hearts from an early age. He hands us talents long before we know exactly how to use them. And the young ones? They aren't afraid to think about those talents, to push into whatever that dream is, to be brave naturally.

I have friends who are sure that life has passed them by, that their opportunity to be brave has come and gone. That is sadder to me than anything—you are not too old! My grandmother was brave until her final breath at the age of eighty-nine.

If you're reading this book, you're alive, and if you're alive, so is a dream.

What are the dreams you can't stop dreaming? Think about that and figure it out because God wants to use that dream. God wants to use that talent. He wants to take your dreams and talents and use them to point others to Him.

I love God. He has meant everything to me in my life. He loves me really well. And let me tell you what one of the ways loving God looks like for me: this right here. Writing. Talking about Him. Expressing my love to Him through the life I live, the people I love, and the causes I serve. I want to live my life in a way that always and forever pumps as much love out of my heart as I can.

If you're reading this book, you're alive, and if you're alive, so is a dream.

Do I make mistakes? Constantly and absolutely. Am I a sinner? You'd better believe it. But every day, for the rest of the time the Lord gives me on earth, I want my entire life to love Him. Through my writing career and any other dreams that God grows in my life and heart.

God loves to put wings on dreams that His kids chase, dreams that can bring Him glory.

BE BRAVE: *What is one dream you hope is still alive in your life?*

Day Thirty

TELL SOMEONE

And let us consider how we may spur one another on toward love and good deeds, not giving up meeting together, as some are in the habit of doing, but encouraging one another—and all the more as you see the Day approaching.

—Hebrews 10:24–25 NIV

At my home church, high school students host and run the middle school retreat. It's a really neat experience. A few years ago, I was an adult leader, and we were at one of those retreat centers that have cabins and bunk beds and two showers for every twenty people. It was as rustic as you are picturing.

On Saturday night of the retreat, I crawled into my little twin bunk, which was shoved up next to another twin bunk, and closed my eyes. It wasn't thirty seconds later that I felt someone tap my shoulder.

Because we are a people who love to prank, I was sure I was about to (1) be sprayed in the face with some sort of liquid or (2) get to participate in pranking someone else. Instead, it was Mallory, a senior helping lead the retreat. She was just a few months away from graduating and heading off to Auburn University.

Mallory asked me to scoot over, so I did. I was worried—was something wrong? Mallory stared up at the springs on the bunk above us. Light from the moon barely snuck in through the curtains, but it was enough for me to watch as she was obviously wrestling with something in her heart.

That little glow of courage was growing in her heart for days, maybe weeks.

"I don't want to go to Auburn," she whispered, and I heard the tears dripping onto my pillow. I waited, thinking she had more to say. When she didn't, I responded.

"Okay, Mal. You don't have to."

"I think," she stammered slowly, "I want to be a missionary. I want to go to YWAM." Her voice was still shaky.

"Okay, Mal. You can do that."

Mallory didn't begin her journey toward courage right there. That little glow of courage had been growing in her heart for days, maybe weeks. And then in the hours and minutes before she actually got up out of her bed, it grew feet, didn't it? Feet that led her to tell someone.

Do you want to be brave? Tell somebody you want to be brave, and then see what God can do.

Be Brave: *Call a friend today. Take him or her to lunch or coffee or meet up and go on a walk. And when y'all are chatting, tell your friend that one brave thing that you haven't said out loud yet.*

Day Thirty-One

HOW DO YOU FIND THE PEOPLE TO TELL?

Without good direction, people lose their way; the more wise counsel you follow, the better your chances.

—Proverbs 11:14 MSG

When it comes to your dreams, you need to guard your heart. Your heart is precious, your dreams should only be shared with a few close friends, and you should love well but carefully. You need to allow love into your heart, but always remember to guard and protect it.

When you're trying to figure out how to find the people you can trust with your dreams, ask yourself a few questions.

1. **Who do I trust?** Think about the people in your life. Does anyone make you feel uneasy? Are there some who always seem to be divulging personal details about other people? Don't pick them.

2. **Who isn't too invested or emotionally involved in my life?** There is absolutely a time to tell your dreams to your core group of people. But telling your core people about a dream you want to

pursue could get hairy. You want to pick someone who wouldn't lose his or her mind hearing, for example, that you might want to move. You want a more objective party.

Your heart is precious, your dreams should only be shared with a few close friends, and you should love well but carefully.

3. **Who have I seen exhibit wisdom in their lives?** Wise people live wise lives. Find them. Watch for them. And then keep them around your life.

4. **Who have I seen repeatedly being trustworthy?** You don't want to share something so intimate and vulnerable with people who don't seem to be very loyal or who don't seem to pursue wisdom.

5. **Who have I seen experience failure?** Yes, you want to share this piece of you with someone successful. Yes, you want your dream to stay safe while it's just a little flicker of something. But, boy oh boy, will you learn a lot from someone who has experienced failure.

Failure is often the best teacher. You might consider sharing your dream with someone who has pursued their dream and achieved it and with someone who mourned that dream and moved on to another.

Be Brave: *Tell someone your dream. Whether you have a huge dream or something smaller, find someone you trust and tell that person.*

Day Thirty-Two

THE DIFFERENCE BETWEEN DREAMS AND CALLING

God's gifts and God's call are under full warranty—never canceled, never rescinded.

—ROMANS 11:29 MSG

I had a pretty vivid dream the other night. It doesn't happen to me often, but when it does, it is visceral. When I woke up, I felt it so deep in my gut that I had to call my friends who were in the dream just to make sure it wasn't a reality. I felt really weird for a few hours, and I had to keep reminding myself that it was just a dream, that none of it had really happened. But that's how dreams work sometimes. They feel very real until they fade away and you return to your normal life.

It doesn't quite go that way when you think about the dreams you have for your life, does it? The dreams I have for my life are often wishes that my heart makes. I dream about a job or a spouse or kids or a house. We can have dreams of things we hope come to pass, things we've seen in our mind's eye, and things we really want to have. And none of that is bad—as long as we keep dreams in their right spot. Not promises, not guarantees, but dreams.

Dreams are different from your calling. Your calling is sure and strong. Your calling, the thing that God has placed in you for the good of the planet and the good of your heart, isn't going anywhere. Rebekah Lyons says your calling is where your burdens and your talents collide.

I think of it this way: your calling is the cash in the bank; your dreams are all the ways you can come up with spending that cash. Another way to look at it? Your calling is the ingredient in the kitchen, and your dreams are all the ways you can use that ingredient.

Your calling, the thing that God has placed in you for the good of the planet and the good of your heart, isn't going anywhere.

Why do we need to differentiate? Because you need to have dreams—big, beautiful, bold, crazy dreams of what you think could happen. But you need to build your life around your calling, not your dreams. Your dreams will change over time. Some will come to pass, and some will pass away. But your calling will remain true.

Be Brave: *Make a list of a few dreams you have for your life. How do you see your calling being displayed in your dreams?*

Brave Enough to Work Hard

Working hard is not for the faint of heart.

Day Thirty-Three

WHAT ARE YOU CREATED TO DO?

I want you to think about how all this makes you more significant, not less. A body isn't just a single part blown up into something huge. It's all the different-but-similar parts arranged and functioning together.

—1 CORINTHIANS 12:14 MSG

What did God create you specifically to do? It's not like you're born knowing the answer to this question. You need to walk through life and stumble and soar and go through all the things and notice what you're drawn to and what doesn't work.

In 1 Corinthians 12, we read about how Christians all have their different parts in the body of Christ. And God is the One who decided what your role in the body would be.

So how do you know what you were created to do? We know, as Christians, that we are all called to point people to Christ. But how are you supposed to do that practically, using your unique makeup?

The answer? Ask God. Spend time in His Word. God is always

speaking to us, to you and to me, and He will speak through His Word. You can also hear God's heart through other people—through your pastor, your small group leader, your parents, and even your friends. I also think that God can whisper truths into your heart through the Holy Spirit.

So how do you know when God is speaking to you?

You learn to recognize the voices of the people you love the most.

Listening to God is a personal thing, to be honest. And I wouldn't dare claim to be an expert. But just like I know my mom's voice when she calls or my friend's voice when she yells at me from across a restaurant, you learn to recognize the voices of the people you love the most.

So practice listening. You can pray something like this: *God, I want to hear from You. Speak to me. Teach me how to hear You in my heart and in what others say to me. Please show me what You want me to do to live out my calling.*

And then wait. And listen. Journal what you hear. Be brave enough to share it with your friends or a mentor you trust. The best way to grow in your ability to hear God is to practice and let others help you.

BE BRAVE: *Take some time today to listen to God. Pray, sit in the quiet, think, and listen. Have your Bible and journal nearby, and see what God has for you today.*

Day Thirty-Four

ONE CALLING

There are different kinds of spiritual gifts, but they all
come from the same Spirit. There are different ways to
serve the same Lord, and we can each do different things.
Yet the same God works in all of us and helps us in everything we do.

—1 Corinthians 12:4–6 cev

When I taught school, my students learned to write five-
paragraph essays. As you probably remember, those include
an opening paragraph, a closing paragraph, and three main
points. Those three points refer back to a thesis statement, which
explains the main point of the essay.

I think our lives look like that. Each of our lives has a thesis
statement—a main thing—one calling.

I've been trying to figure out what my thesis statement is when
it comes to my calling because it can have different points. I think
my thesis statement, so far, has been: *I'm the friend who entertains
you long enough that you learn something.*

I have a friend named Jason, and he's the bass player for a

Christian artist. But he's also their tour manager, which feels like two really different jobs. Like, one of them is playing an instrument onstage, and the other one is making sure everyone knows what time the tour bus is leaving. But the truth is, his thesis statement is that he keeps everybody in line. He has figured out what he's good at. Just as a bass player is part of the percussion and keeps the rhythm, his calling is to help people stay in line.

Jobs will come and go. Your calling won't.

Jesus was a carpenter, *and He was our Savior.* Jesus takes raw materials and turns them into things that matter. Jesus can take something broken and make it right. And it's not because He had two different jobs. They are different expressions of His calling. Different points to His thesis.

Jobs will come and go. Your calling won't. Whether it's mothering or mentoring, teaching, nursing, building. It's not what you do but how you do it.

The ways you express your calling are different. So ask God to help you find yours. Remember that there are many different kinds of gifts, but God is the Source of them all. Don't be afraid to try out a different expression of your calling. Don't let fear of failure keep you from what God wants you to do.

BE BRAVE: *Work on writing a thesis statement for your life. What would you say is the theme of all the jobs, dreams, and opportunities you've had in your life?*

Day Thirty-Five

MULTIPLE EXPRESSIONS

With my whole heart I seek you; let me not wander from
your commandments!

—Psalm 119:10 esv

Maybe you've taken the last few days to figure out your calling.
Maybe God has given you a clear picture and you're exploring what that looks like in your life.

As you sort through this with the Lord, don't listen to the enemy when he tries to discourage you. Hear this—you are not too old to figure out your calling, and you're not too young to have already had multiple expressions of it.

Before the writing and the speaking and the books and the travel, I taught elementary school. It's actually the job I *always* dreamed of. I have vivid memories of second and third grade, particularly my teacher Miss Albers. I *loved* her. I remember leaving third grade and thinking, *This is who I want to be. This is what I want to do.*

And almost immediately from that point on, I pursued being a teacher. I went to the University of Georgia, I studied teaching, and then I taught elementary school. I *loved it.*

I particularly loved it during the winter, when the bulletin-board designs were awesome and the parties . . . I know, I know. It shocks you that I would be the teacher who was like, "I like the parties!" I mean, I guess I liked the kids learning things too.

I've had two full careers. Two very different careers. But my calling has always been the same.

I loved reading books out loud to them. I loved being in their everyday lives. It was a dream job. While I was doing that, I was also volunteering with my local church's youth group, and I started writing curriculum for them. Then one day our youth pastor was sick and asked me to teach. And all of this snowballed until I had these two competing careers. I would go home from school and write all night and drink all the caffeine from all the caffeine stops on my way to school the next day.

And I felt like God put this opportunity in front of me and was like, "Hey. This writing and speaking thing. You want to try?"

So God asked me if I wanted to be brave, and I said yes.

I've had two full careers. Two very different careers. But my calling has always been the same.

I believe that we all have one calling, but it can be expressed in lots of ways. One calling. Multiple expressions. Be brave and explore them.

BE BRAVE: *Is God revealing some different ways you might express your calling?*

Day Thirty-Six

WORK IN PIECES

The plans of the diligent lead surely to abundance, but everyone who is hasty comes only to poverty.

—Proverbs 21:5 esv

When I was teaching elementary school, I wasn't dreaming of writing books. I could barely imagine writing out the story of how I wanted to tell stories! Then I started a blog that took courage every day to write.

I worked on that piece of my puzzle.

Then I wrote a Bible study for a group of high school girls who came over to my house on Monday nights.

That was the next piece.

Then those printed-out lessons became *Perfectly Unique*, a book read by thousands of girls around the world. And then came my next book, *Speak Love*. And then *Let's All Be Brave*. And then *Looking for Lovely* . . . and then whichever one comes after this one (that I promise won't start with an *L*).

In order to get to each of those pieces, I had to be brave enough to work where I was. Even if I could dream bigger or wish for a different situation, I knew the thing to do was write and speak right where I was, to be brave in the spot God had placed me.

And now we are here. You and I. And we are fighting against fear.

So what should you do today?

Do what's right in front of you.

If your dream is to someday be the presi-

Do what's right in front of you.

dent of your company, don't show up late to work every day now as an employee. Do your best today, in whatever spot or position you're in. That will take you to the next piece.

Just like today's verse says, good planning and hard work lead to prosperity. If you want to enjoy the fruit of working out of your calling, put in the hard work right where you are today. Work in pieces.

BE BRAVE: *Looking at your life today, what's one piece of your calling you can see on display?*

Day Thirty-Seven

WHERE CAN YOUR CALLING TAKE YOU?

God can do anything, you know—far more than you could
ever imagine or guess or request in your wildest dreams!
He does it not by pushing us around but by working within
us, his Spirit deeply and gently within us.

—Ephesians 3:20 msg

*L*et's say you're working on a piece of your puzzle. You know what
your calling is. You know that what you're doing now, whether
it's professionally or in your spare time, is working on a piece
of the bigger thing you feel called to do. Maybe you know what that
thing is. Or maybe you don't. Or maybe you've changed your mind!

I can't tell you the number of people I know who changed majors
in college. Or who went to school for one thing and wound up doing
something totally different.

What's cool about your calling is that there are no dead ends.
Even if you weren't brave enough to pursue your last opportunity,
you can be brave this time.

Where can your calling take you? It's unlimited! If you're not sure what this looks like for you, be brave enough to sit some people down and say, "Hey. Help me, please?"

One of my Nashville friends did this. He's been a musician forever, but he wasn't sure he still wanted to do it anymore. So he invited a bunch of us to his house to eat dinner and say to him, "These are some other strengths I see in you. What if your calling looked like _____. Like this. And this—and this—and this—and this."

What's cool about your calling is that there are no dead ends. Even if you weren't brave enough to pursue your last opportunity, you can be brave this time.

He wasn't asking us to help find his calling. He was asking us to help him find other expressions of it. He knew his calling. But was he doing it for fun or for financial means? What else could he be doing?

Inviting people into those deeper questions of your heart can feel scary. What if they say something you don't want to hear? Be brave enough to listen. Be brave enough to disagree.

Where will your calling take you? God knows, and if you're brave, soon you will too.

Be Brave: *As you seek out where your calling could take you, who could you invite into this conversation? Who do you trust with your dreams and stories that can help you brainstorm?*

Day Thirty-Eight

WHEN YOUR CALLING ISN'T YOUR JOB

Whatever you do, work heartily, as for the Lord and not for men.

—Colossians 3:23 esv

What about when you're stuck in a job that isn't what you're forever called to do? There are times when you're doing a job that is not your calling. Maybe it's nowhere near your calling. Maybe you feel like every hour that you work at your job, you're doing the opposite of your calling.

In those situations, you are still called to be faithful with your work—working as for the Lord and not for men.

I've had jobs that weren't my calling. I mean, working at the Local Taco was not my calling (even though it was delicious), but I needed to make money. So I showed up to work on time, I did the right things, I did the best I could until I didn't work there anymore, and I gained a ton from that experience.

Hardly anyone goes from realizing their dreams to discovering their calling to getting to do their perfect dream job. We all have parts of our jobs that aren't our favorite, but we have to do them.

When I was still figuring out what my career was going to look like, I was really poor—I mean, barely getting by, having to ask my parents for money, carpooling to save gas, selling-things-on-Craigslist poor. And so were a lot of my friends. At that time, many of us were on the first few steps of our creative careers, and those first few steps looked like shuffling in the porridge line with Oliver Twist. I nannied. I worked at the Local Taco. I took jobs I found online for editing or writing copy.

Hardly anyone goes from realizing their dreams to discovering their calling to getting to do their perfect dream job.

I was hustling. And I had to. And I never would have been able to make it, doing what I do now, what I love, if I hadn't worked hard at those jobs that weren't my calling.

You've got to be brave enough to be faithful, even when you don't want to be. You've got to be brave to work hard now for a payoff that won't come until later. But it is so worth it!

Be Brave: *Do something at your job today that takes a little courage. Suggest a new idea. Try something creative. Speak to someone you usually avoid.*

Day Thirty-Nine

>>>>

FIND YOUR CALLING AT YOUR JOB

Therefore, my dear brothers and sisters, stand firm. Let nothing move you. Always give yourselves fully to the work of the Lord, because you know that your labor in the Lord is not in vain.

—1 CORINTHIANS 15:58 NIV

Let's talk more about my stint at the Local Taco because, thanks to good Mexican food, I was still able to operate in my calling there (and eat delicious tacos on the regular).

If my calling is to entertain people long enough that they learn something, I could do that at the Local Taco! I helped people figure out what tasted good and sort through the options, all while feeling like they are talking to a friend. I was just me, doing the job that was right in front of me.

You can be fully you wherever you are. And it's your choice.

So are you brave enough to find your calling at your not-quite-it job?

Let's say your dream is to be a nurse. Are you brave enough to say, "I've always dreamed of being a nurse because I love taking care of people. And here I am working at a restaurant. But, hey, I still can take care of people. I can't save their lives, but I can take care of my coworkers and take care of my customers."

You can be fully you wherever you are. And it's your choice.

Can you look around the life you have and find ways that your calling is already there, even if your job doesn't look the way you thought it would look?

No matter who signs your paychecks, God believes in you. He believes in all the ways He made you unique. He believes in all the dreams bubbling inside your heart. He believes in your ability to take hold of the tiny ledge that is your next call to courage.

I believe in you too. I believe you picked up this book for a reason and the idea that your life could be different after 100 days of focusing on courage matters to you. You want to be brave. In your middle place—I like to call it the "knower," somewhere between your chest and your backbone—you know you want to be brave.

You can be brave and find your calling no matter what your job is now and no matter where you may work in the future. You are one of a kind, made on purpose, deeply loved, and called to be courageous.

BE BRAVE: *Can you list a few reasons that the job you have today is the exact right one for this season?*

Day Forty

WORK HARD

Hard work always pays off; mere talk puts no bread on the table.

—Proverbs 14:23 MSG

Persevere. Work hard. Don't be wimpy.

I'm a part of the millennial generation. And people have, as they do with all generations, stereotyped us a bit. Among the good and the bad, one thing millennials are known for is not working as hard as our parents did. And listen, I've gotta be honest. I don't love to work hard all the time.

I don't know about you, and I don't know what generation you're a part of and what that generation is known for, but I don't want to feed this perception of my generation.

I want to be punctual. In fact, I want to be about three minutes early. When I say I'll be there, I want to be there, wherever "there" happens to be.

Our new intern, Haile, started on the same day the office microwave broke. She didn't break it; she just happened to arrive on the day the glass on the front shattered into one billion pieces. I had a meeting that afternoon, and as I was leaving, I just mentioned to her, "Be careful when you walk by this. I'll clean it up when I get back."

When I returned home two hours later, Haile had cleaned up all the glass. It was not in her job description. I didn't ask her to do it. She just saw a little bit of hard work that needed to get done, and she did it. And she wasn't just trying to impress us on her first day. That's who Haile continued to be for the whole internship (which is why we hired her once she graduated from college).

> *Whatever you're doing and whatever you're asked to do, work hard.*

I saw courage in her, to step into a mess she didn't make and work hard to clean it up. I was impressed. Still am.

You gain a lot when you work really hard. You gain respect. You get to keep your job. You gain a good reputation. It isn't always fun, but it's who you want to be, isn't it? Don't you want to be a person who is known for working hard?

Whatever you're doing and whatever you're asked to do, work hard. It really does pay off.

Be Brave: *Work hard today, friend. Seriously. Give more than you have, and see what comes from it.*

Day Forty-One

WHO YOU DO LIFE WITH MATTERS AS MUCH AS WHAT YOU DO

As iron sharpens iron, so one person sharpens another.

—Proverbs 27:17 NIV

When you're picking a job or going after your calling, if you abandon all the people who matter, then you've missed out on how to do this well.

We see that all the time, right? People work super hard and put in fifteen-hour days, but they don't have any friends or they go home to broken families.

We've got to be brave enough to find balance. Even if there's financial pressure (there usually is, isn't there?). Even if there's pressure at work. We have to be brave enough to balance work and life because we need relationships.

In the early days of my Nashville life, I developed a group of friends who became like family. We were all very low on funds (some would say "broke"), and we all wanted to be together. No one wanted to eat alone, but we couldn't afford to eat out.

And so began family dinner.

Our Sunday ritual started out simple enough. Much like the classic children's tale *Stone Soup*, we all brought what meager things we could to scrounge together a decent meal. Jason brought a pound of ground beef. While Laura browned it, Emily chopped an onion. We boiled noodles and added carrots (thank you, Claire) and a variety of fresh garden veggies (from Joel, who is a famous songwriter, so he was rich enough to buy fresh vegetables). And with a lot of water, that soup satisfied us.

We've got to be brave enough to find balance.

Evan makes the meanest grilled cheese sandwich this side of the Mississippi. Thanks to Betsy, who brought a block of sharp cheddar cheese; Marisa, who provided a loaf of bread; and my garlic salt, we all ate our fill.

I relaxed into that family spot like it had always been mine. And week after week, we ate together.

It wasn't always a perfect setup. When you fill a family with young artists pursuing their dreams, emotions tend to run higher than usual (creatives are known for that) and people get their feelings hurt. There were times when friends got left out or too many people showed up but forgot food to share, so there wasn't enough to feed everyone. But for months, our tradition lived. We made room for each other every week. We prioritized each other—with our time, our money, and our groceries.

Friends, we all need that. Don't let pursuing your dreams or maximizing your calling keep you from investing in relationships. Share your life with others.

Be Brave: *Eat dinner with someone tonight. Call a friend. Text your family. Find someone to hang out with, and share your story with that person.*

Brave Enough to
Love Others

It takes guts to love.

Day Forty-Two

>>>> ——————

BRAVE PEOPLE
NEED PEOPLE

You are better off to have a friend than to be all alone, because then you will get more enjoyment out of what you
earn. If you fall, your friend can help you up. But if you fall
without having a friend nearby, you are really in trouble.

—ECCLESIASTES 4:9–10 CEV

One Fourth of July, I was exactly one week from moving from
Nashville to Edinburgh, Scotland. I was terribly sad to leave my
community. I knew God had said to go to Edinburgh. I just was
brokenhearted to leave my people.

So on that sunny day in July, our crew spent the day tubing down
the Buffalo River. We laughed as people got flipped out of their tubes
by rapids, and we brought enough snacks to float all the way to Florida
and never get hungry or thirsty. It began to rain, and we laughed again
as everything we had worked so hard to keep dry got soaked. It was one
of those bookmark days, the kind you will tell your kids about.

We got back home just in time to clean up and reconvene for

the fireworks show. Walking toward the parking deck to get a good look at the fireworks, we were just a friendship amoeba—a blob of people. To my left, Curt—a production manager for a local band and one of the most responsible and kind men in my life. To my right, Lyndsay—a fantastic writer and one of my best friends.

As the tears began to puddle right on top of my lower eyelids, I slid my left hand into the bend of Curt's right elbow. We smiled. The tears rolled slowly down my cheeks. If there was a way to stop them, I didn't know it and couldn't have thought through those steps clearly anyway. I said to Lynds, "Hold my hand." And so we walked, the three of us, linked by my sorrow, to see a fireworks show.

I knew with my whole heart that God wanted me to move, but I mourned leaving my people. As sad as that part of my life was, I wouldn't trade it for the world.

It's easier to have a relationship with your Netflix queue. Why? Because you don't have to say any painful good-byes. You don't have any friction with your Netflix shows. If you don't like a show, you drop it. But friendship takes work. Friendship takes courage.

We all need people. You've got to be brave and let yourself love people. And to make brave choices, you have got to have the support of your own friendship amoeba.

Friendship takes work. Friendship takes courage.

BE BRAVE: *Send a letter to a friend who has been there for you before. Thank him or her. Tell your friend how much he or she means to you.*

Day Forty-Three

YOUR FAMILY

Long, long ago he decided to adopt us into his family through Jesus Christ. (What pleasure he took in planning this!) He wanted us to enter into the celebration of his lavish gift-giving by the hand of his beloved Son.

—Ephesians 1:5 MSG

Every family has its own unique makeup, strengths, and pains. For many people, loving your family, or just being in your family *period*, can take more courage than any of your other relationships combined.

But God does family perfectly. He adopted us, flawed and often unhealthy, into His family through Jesus. He loves us even when we aren't lovely. It doesn't mean that we are required to do family perfectly; it just means that we are treated and cared for perfectly in *His* family.

So what does it mean to be brave in your family? It means that you can be brave enough to love your family well even if your family isn't always healthy. It means that you can be brave enough to stay in family and to love family and to create family.

There's this great book called *Hillbilly Elegy*, and if you haven't read it yet, oh my goodness. Fix that soon, please. It's a story about a guy who grew up in rural Appalachia and ended up going to Yale and creating a successful life for himself. He broke the generational norm and created something new.

But one of my takeaways from the book (because I'm always thinking about courage, right?) was—*Oh my gosh! He didn't come from a healthy family (though he does a great job honoring them in his book), but he was brave enough to build his own. He has a wife and has kids . . . I think he has kids. He has dogs, at least.*

You can be brave enough to love your family well even if your family isn't always healthy.

Here's where I'm going with this: Are you brave enough to build a family even if you had problems in your nuclear family?

And what does it look like to love your family well even if they've hurt you? Every situation is different, of course. Sometimes the best way to love certain family members is from a distance.

What might this look like for you? It's following the example of God, who lives and breathes forgiveness and grace. It's asking Him for wisdom with those in your family who baffle you. Pray for the courage to stick with your family and love them as they are, the way God has loved you.

BE BRAVE: *Call someone in your family. Thank this person for his or her love and support through the years. Maybe family is complicated for you; I get that. Then call someone who has been like family to you.*

Day Forty-Four

YOUR FRIENDS

Love one another with brotherly affection. Outdo one another in showing honor.

—ROMANS 12:10 ESV

R ememember when I told you in Day 41 about my "family dinners" with my friends? Well, our family dinner crew hadn't all been together in years, but many of us found each other again last December, around bowls of chili and tables and couches and stories and laughs.

There are more of us than there were seven years ago because of some excellent additions of spouses and children. But it was like we hadn't missed any time together at all. Conversations lasted for hours, friendships were regrown, and lots of food was consumed. Over the next few days, many of us discussed how much we needed that night. About the longevity of the friendships and the history we had together.

I know I sound like a broken record about this, but *you need friends*. I need friends. They need you.

You need to be brave and let people get close enough to speak into your life. The gift of community is so sweet, but you have to be brave and let down your defenses to develop those relationships in your life.

Romans 12:10 tells us to outdo one another in showing honor. Love like that will change you. It will change them.

You need to be brave and let people get close enough to speak into your life.

Eating chili with old friends at Christmas was so great. That thing holding us together—whatever kept a bunch of poor, single friends making dinners together on Sunday nights all those years ago—is still there. We're still us. And I'm a better Annie because of those humans and those dinners. My cup runneth over for sure.

I'm so thankful that they were brave enough to let me into their lives and that I was brave enough to let them into mine.

BE BRAVE: *Pick up your phone and call a friend you haven't seen in a while.*

Day Forty-Five

DATING AND MARRIAGE

Trust GOD from the bottom of your heart; don't try to figure out everything on your own. Listen for GOD's voice in
everything you do, everywhere you go; he's the one who
will keep you on track.

—PROVERBS 3:5–6 MSG

I stood in my friends Rob and Emily's guest bathroom, getting ready
for a date I didn't want to go on. Rob was watching golf, and I was
putting on my makeup and trying to get my four billion hairs in
some sort of organized fashion.

As I continued to get ready, Rob asked me lots of questions: Who
is this guy? How did you meet him? Why did you say yes?

Before the inquisition was over, I was crying.

I didn't want to go on this date. I had only stopped dating a
wonderful guy a few weeks before, and "getting back out there" felt
like pouring salt in a wound in hopes it would heal.

But I said yes. It was a fine date. We had good conversation, and
he thought I was really funny, so that always goes far in my heart. We
never went out again.

Going on a date with an acquaintance didn't fix everything. I was still sad. It didn't bring healing. But it did build something good in me—the knowledge that life was going to go on. I was going to be okay.

I've never regretted being brave enough to put myself out there and try.

I've been on bad dates, and I've been on great dates that turned into relationships. And of course there are people and moments that bring back painful memories, but I've never regretted being brave enough to put myself out there and try.

If you're not married yet, go on dates. Seriously. Put yourself out there, friend. You just have to go for it, even when it's scary or unknown.

You will learn things about God's love and personality from friendship, dating, and marriage, and fear will try to keep you from giving your heart in those relationships. Don't let fear win.

Married friends, keep being brave in your marriage. Give your spouse grace. Be brave enough to be open and communicate your feelings. Don't let the years of hurts and pain put a wall between you. Don't run away when you feel rejected.

Be brave enough to stick with it. Brave enough to forgive and be forgiven.

BE BRAVE: *Oh, y'all are gonna love this one. Married friends, ask your spouse on a date. Single friends, ask someone to coffee. Like, someone who could be someone. Be brave. Go for it! It's just coffee.*

Day Forty-Six

>>>>——————>

YOUR CHURCH

Love is patient and kind; love does not envy or boast; love does not parade itself, is not puffed up; does not behave rudely, does not seek its own, is not provoked, thinks no evil; does not rejoice in iniquity, but rejoices in the truth; bears all things, believes all things, hopes all things, endures all things.

—1 Corinthians 13:4–7 esv

I don't know where you are in your church walk and your church story. Maybe you recently started following Jesus and the church is still totally your jam. I'm so glad for you, but here's some truth. Just like any relationship, you and the church will have rocky times. Just like any relationship, at some point the flawed humans who lead your church will disappoint you, and you will need to put 1 Corinthians 13 love into action.

You know why church is hard? Because of humans. So. Many. Humans.

My local church recently went through something hard, and to be honest, my feelings were all over the place. I didn't want to stay.

I once asked my friend Pastor Scott Sauls what happens when

you stay in a church even when you are hurt or it seems hard. He said, "That's when you grow up."

Wow.

Part of being a Christian is wrestling through Scripture and wrestling through relationships. If we unplug ourselves from the local church, we don't even wrestle. We lose the opportunity to wrestle inside so that you love well outside.

You know why church is hard? Because of humans. So. Many. Humans.

When we're outside of our Christian community, we are called to love well. To outdo one another in kindness. To put others before ourselves. If we unplug from our church, we're unplugging from our family of believers. Our support system.

Brave Christians get plugged in to their church. And brave people are willing to stay plugged in, even when things get hard.

BE BRAVE: *This Sunday, go to church. If you don't know a good one, call someone and ask. If you've been hurt, go back anyway—to the one you know or one you don't. But step back through the doors and see what happens next.*

Day Forty-Seven

>>>>———

FIND A MENTOR

Walk with the wise and become wise, for a companion of
fools suffers harm.

—Proverbs 13:20 NIV

Finding a mentor seems like a scary thought, but it's really not.
There isn't some weird mentor ceremony with pins and smoke
machines and lifelong commitments. It really doesn't have to
be that intense.

But it takes bravery to put yourself out there and ask someone
to give you some of his or her wisdom. People are busy these days. I
know I am. I bet you are too.

Are you brave enough to ask someone?

Just to calm your fears a little, here is what asking for a mentor
does *not* look like: you walking up to someone and saying, "You are
my mentor" or "God told me that you are my mentor."

No. Please, no.

I'll make it really simple for you. Find someone you respect in
your life who is two or three steps ahead of you, someone you can
go to dinner with and ask the hard questions.

You don't have to label someone a *mentor* for that person to be mentoring you. It doesn't have to be one single person who becomes your guru. And it doesn't have to be a biweekly commitment.

You can have multiple mentors for different areas of your life. A work mentor. A family mentor. A calling mentor.

It takes bravery to put yourself out there and ask someone to give you some of his or her wisdom.

Don't shy away from asking because you feel like you'll be a burden.

I've spent a lot of my adult life mentoring college students, and I absolutely love it. During my seasons of mentoring and discipling and hanging out with young adults on a regular basis, I was the happiest, most fulfilled Annie ever.

You will reap crazy benefits from inviting mentors into your life, but so will they. Being used by God in that way is an honor.

So be brave. Ask. Don't build it up into a huge thing. Don't ask one person to be your guru. But do invite people in and learn from their wisdom.

BE BRAVE: *Invite an older, wiser person to grab coffee with you this week.*

Day Forty-Eight

YOUR ONLINE LIFE

"You are the light of the world. A city set on a hill cannot be hidden. Nor do people light a lamp and put it under a basket, but on a stand, and it gives light to all in the house. In the same way, let your light shine before others, so that they may see your good works and give glory to your Father who is in heaven."

—MATTHEW 5:14–16 ESV

You've Got Mail is still my favorite movie. Maybe it's because the main character owns a tiny bookstore, or maybe it's the overuse of twinkly lights, daisies, tissues, and knee-length skirts, but if that movie comes on television, I can hardly walk away.

Back when it first came out, the idea that you would meet a person on the Internet was so foreign and creepy that it forged new territory. That is no longer true. The Internet keeps us together, and I'm grateful. On its best-behaved days, I've seen the Internet be the string that ties together old friendships that might otherwise break apart.

Today's verse is about being the light of the world. We are to be a light wherever we go, even online.

Before I started writing books, I began as a blogger (anniefdowns

.com/blog). When I first started, I knew about five people with a blog. I just started writing for those five. For my friends. I began to tell stories of my days in the classroom as an elementary school teacher, my church experiences, and the ridiculous things that seem to happen to me a lot. And before I knew it, strangers were reading what I wrote.

My blog audience has watched my life unfold firsthand, and my light, while sometimes foggy and often dim and flawed, has shown over the city of people who come to my website every time I write a blog post. And God is glorified, even in my mistakes. Readers don't have to really know me for them to experience God through my life.

We are to be a light wherever we go, even online.

The medium doesn't matter. Facebook. Twitter. Blog. Instagram. Pinterest. (I'm @anniefdowns in all the places if you want to connect!) You have so many chances to share light, to share God, to make Him known to the people who listen to your voice. But the Internet is not exactly a Christ-welcoming place. It takes courage to share your faith and be a light for Jesus, whether you're online or not. We need to view technology as tools God gave us to glorify Him, however that looks and however many "unfollows" it costs us. Let's all be brave with our online platforms.

BE BRAVE: *Take a picture of the cover of this book, and post it on your social media spots. Offer for your friends to join you in this 100-day challenge. Make sure to use the hashtag #100daystobrave!*

Day Forty-Nine

YOUR WORDS MATTER

In the beginning, God created the heavens and the earth. The earth was without form and void, and darkness was over the face of the deep. And the Spirit of God was hovering over the face of the waters. And God said, "Let there be light," and there was light.

—Genesis 1:1–3 ESV

If we go back to the book of Genesis, where the world began, we see that God started it all with words. He spoke, and things came into being. Light. Land. Lizards. All with a word. And we are made in His image.

God was brave enough to make you, brave enough to make me, brave enough to make humans who would all break His heart.

Proverbs 18:21 tells us that our tongues have the power of life and death, which we talked about on Day 12. I see that in my life. I see that in my friendships. I see that in the memories of past things said to me.

If there are seeds of courage living in all of us, waiting to bloom, words are the sun and the water that cheer on those seeds to their fullness.

One spring a few years ago, I pressured about ten of my girl-friends to buy a month's membership to a boot camp. We were going to get fit before the summer if it killed us.

(To be noted—it almost killed me.)

It was no regular boot camp. It was a boot camp outside at 5:00 a.m. about twenty minutes from our neighborhood. So each of us had to wake up in the early 4:00s and then go exercise before the sun was even up.

As the month went on, the teacher realized a couple of things about me: (1) I did not enjoy being there, and (2) I am the class clown almost always.

So in typical teacher-versus–class clown behavior, she started putting me at the front of the line or calling on me to lead the stretches or staring at me all too often. I hated it. As much as I love being the center of attention, I do not prefer it when I'm exercising. *Leave me alone and let me do my forty squats in peace, lady.*

If there are seeds of courage living in all of us, waiting to bloom, words are the sun and the water that cheer on those seeds to their fullness.

On one of the last days of boot camp, we had to complete an obstacle course. As was the case every day, I was the last person to finish. The end of the course was a sprint around cones while holding a weighted ball. I began, and the teacher ran beside me, absolutely screaming in my ears.

"You can do this, Annie! Don't quit now. You are so close! You wouldn't have made it this far a few days ago! Finish strong!"

As much as I hate to admit this, it worked. Her words in my ear gave me the push I needed to complete the course, get in my car, and never go back to boot camp again.

(Just kidding. I went back for the last two days.)

My point is, words matter. God wants you to use your words to encourage and speak life. Ask Him for the grace to do so, and look for opportunities to be brave, speaking truth and love into a broken world.

Be Brave: *Who can you encourage today? Who needs to know that you are cheering for them? Do it!*

Day Fifty

WHEN RELATIONSHIPS CHANGE

I lift up my eyes to the mountains—where does my help come from? My help comes from the LORD, the Maker of heaven and earth.

—PSALM 121:1–2 NIV

Every relationship changes. That's a hard reality, one that absolutely requires me to lift my eyes up and let the Lord help me through it. Because, honestly, I just do not like change.

As a single girl, I've had a few breakups, and they are never fun. Whether you are on the giving or receiving end of a breakup, it hurts. You think if you are the dumped, the other person is fine. But if you've ever been the dumper, you know that's not the case.

Breakups are gross and sad and such a unique pain. We can talk through every side until you've heard every he-said/she-said detail, actual or fabricated, and even then the pain will still be there.

But you know what we don't talk about enough? When friendships break up.

Of all the romantic breakups in my life, none have come close to hurting the way a breakup with a best friend hurts. I didn't know a feeling like that could exist. It was breathtaking, but in an absolutely terrible way.

And after the dust settled, I didn't know who to talk with and I didn't know what to feel and I didn't know what to call the thing that had just happened. What do you do when things are broken with your person?

Of all the romantic breakups in my life, none have come close to hurting the way a breakup with a best friend hurts.

You lift your eyes up to God—your Helper. Your Comforter. Your Father. Your Friend.

Jesus cares and He understands. He allowed His relationship with His Father to be broken for you. He can empathize.

This may sound cliché, but trust me. I'm doing it *today*. I'm choosing to trust God and His heart and that His eyes are still on this, even though I feel a friendship changing in ways I didn't see coming. It's a little painful, a little scary, but trust in this is the brave choice.

If your relationship is changing in a way that is heartbreaking, don't try to distract the pain away. Be brave enough to let Jesus into the ripped places.

BE BRAVE: *Do you see a relationship in your life changing? Write about it. Ask God to show you where He is in the midst of this change.*

BRAVE ENOUGH
TO FACE CHANGE

Change always comes.

Day Fifty-One

CHANGE ALWAYS HAPPENS

Every good and perfect gift is from above, coming down from the Father of the heavenly lights, who does not change like shifting shadows.

—JAMES 1:17 NIV

Everything you have, from your health to your friendships to a roof over your head to the food in your belly, is a gift from God. And we even have something else to be thankful for: that God doesn't change! I love that about Him.

We can hold tight to our never-changing God and be okay because, in every other area of life, change is pretty much guaranteed. And you know what? Brave people are willing to let go of everything as they hold tight to God, even when things start to change.

In the last three months, I have seen the most change in my personal and professional life that I've ever had. For my counselor, I listed every North Star person (you know, a person who is important to you and gives you guidance) who has left my life in the last three months, and the number is seven. Seven.

And you know what? It's okay.

If I chose to live in a world where I hated change all the time, I would be really miserable. If I chose to put all my hope in people, I would be really miserable. (I've tried both. It's always miserable.)

Brave people are willing to let go of everything as they hold tight to God, even when things start to change.

I don't love change, but I know that God is always working for my good. So I can say, "Man, this is the worst!" But I have a totally trustworthy God who is looking out for me.

Does God need a reminder that He has all this under control? No, friend. He doesn't. You do. I definitely do. We all do.

Remembering that He's the boss and His plans are for our good and He loves us? That can make us brave, even when everything that felt secure seems to be changing.

BE BRAVE: *List a few changes you've seen in your life lately. How are you seeing God use these changes to shape you?*

Day Fifty-Two

>>>>----

PREPARE FOR CHANGE

Jesus Christ is the same yesterday and today and forever.
—Hebrews 13:8 niv

We never get shocked when the seasons change. Like, when summer goes to fall, I'm not surprised. Why? Because I look at calendars and notice the weather patterns and see the advertisements that are telling me to *buy boots*. I can prepare. I do prepare. When winter comes, we make sure we have boots and a coat, right? Because we're always prepared for that change.

Can we do that in our physical, emotional, and spiritual lives too?

I'm right on the heels of a season that was pretty much defined by nothing but change. All summer long, the Lord was like, "Change is coming . . . change is coming."

I even wrote it in my journal. Multiple times.

And as the seasons have played out, I've thought, *Oh. You're really kind to me, God.* I was mentally prepared for change, because God told me to be, so when the change actually happened, it didn't send me into a pit.

So where does our bravery play into this?

Look at today's verse. Whatever change may be coming, Jesus never changes. We can be brave because Jesus is constant, even when our circumstances are not.

I need that reminder—that just as the seasons change on earth, they are going to change in my life. And when I start to sense that little bit of shift, like *Just as the seasons change on earth, they are going to change in my life.* the first hints of fall or the first hot summer day that always comes on the backside of spring, I have to prepare and see it coming and know it's all part of the journey.

How do you prepare?

Spend time in God's Word. Spend time talking to Him—the unchanging One. Trust Him, keep your eyes on Him, and walk out the path. Let the seasons change, and let your heart change with them.

BE BRAVE: *Write a prayer to God, thanking Him that He does not change.*

Day Fifty-Three

>>> ———

SMALL DECISIONS MATTER

What a person plants, he will harvest.

—GALATIANS 6:7 MSG

When you're going through change, small decisions matter.

Going to the gym a few times a week isn't going to change your life immediately, but it's going to matter. Going to the gym even once a week probably doesn't feel like a brave choice, but it is. Because a little yes can be a step in the right direction, even if it isn't a leap.

It's important to make good small decisions when you're in the midst of change because they matter.

You know, small decisions don't feel very brave in the moment. When you think of being brave, you probably think of giant leaps. Grand gestures. Those are clearly brave. But it's also brave to be intentional to make small, healthy decisions because it goes against our human nature to put effort into things that are seemingly insignificant.

The cowardly way to live is to unplug, not to care, to say, "It doesn't matter . . ." It's brave to make small decisions with the big picture in mind.

Little yeses lead to big yeses.

Looking at the importance of small decisions from another angle, saying little noes along the way allows you to do great things. Saying little noes that give you some space in your life allows other things to grow.

It's just like a garden. You can't say yes to every seed. You can only garden certain things because if you said yes to every seed available, there would not be space for things to grow.

When you look at your life, what are the parts of it that, if they grew, would bring glory to God? What fulfills you? What's healthy for your heart? Ask God these questions. And as you pan out and look at the big picture of your life, don't take any small decision lightly.

A little yes can be a step in the right direction, even if it isn't a leap.

BE BRAVE: *Make a small decision today—a conversation, a meal, an e-mail. Do one little brave thing and see how it changes your day.*

Day Fifty-Four

>>>> ———————➤

SAY YES

The righteous are as bold as a lion.

—Proverbs 28:1 NIV

Saying yes changes everything. Walking through the door, agreeing in the moment. Sometimes it is just what is needed to show you the next big yes. I said yes to interning at UGA. I said yes to moving back to Marietta. I said yes to Nashville. I said yes to Scotland. I said yes to college ministry in Nashville after returning from Scotland, in a major life-circle kind of way.

We have to say yes. Even when it's scary or costly or unknown. We don't screw up by saying yes to the wrong things; we screw up by letting all the floats in the parade pass us by and never jumping on one of them for a ride to the end.

Moving to India to start an orphanage as a single woman. Giving up your solo music career to join a group of unguaranteed success. Giving up the life you know as a single person to get married.

You've heard before that saying yes to one thing is saying no to all the others. It's true, I think. If I say yes to a sushi dinner with my Vanderbilt baseball players, I'm saying no to Mexican with my friends. If I say yes to a city, a date, or a friend in need, I'm saying no to all the other options.

If the yeses feel scary, take comfort in knowing that if you are seeking God, if you are asking Him to lead you, He hears you and is doing just that! If you are living in obedience to Him, and He brings opportunities into your life, you can trust that He will take care of you when you say yes.

Say yes to the situations that stretch you and scare you and ask you to be a better you than you think you can be.

Say yes to the gym. Say yes to the open door. Say yes to the situations that stretch you and scare you and ask you to be a better you than you think you can be. Say yes to the moments that will only come once. Say yes to serving. Say yes to Jesus in every way—every chance you get.

BE BRAVE: *Say yes to one small thing today—a friend's request, a push from the Lord, an invite to an event, a healthy choice for yourself.*

Day Fifty-Five

>>>> ————————→

SAY NO

But even if he does not [rescue us], we want you to know,
Your Majesty, that we will not serve your gods or worship
the image of gold you have set up.

—DANIEL 3:18 NIV

You may have heard me talk about this before, but I am deeply moved by the story of Shadrach, Meshach, and Abednego in Daniel 3. These young Israelite men were captured as slaves when they were just teenagers and taken to Babylon with Daniel.

In Daniel 1, we see them say no to meats and rich foods for ten days, and at the end of it, they are honored for their strength, especially in the face of eating much less than the other soldiers in training.

Years later, those young men were administrators over all of Babylon, and Daniel was serving at the royal court. King Nebuchadnezzar built a massive gold statue—ninety feet high, nine feet wide. And then he decided that everyone in town had to bow to the statue and worship it whenever the music played, and anyone who didn't would be thrown into a blazing furnace.

Our guys worshipped the one true God and had no interest in bowing to anything else. They said no when the rest of the people said yes.

Can you imagine that courage? To stand when everyone else bows? Knowing the result, knowing who you are and how much you are respected, yet choosing to go against your boss, namely, *the king*, in a life-threatening way?

Look at today's verse. "Even if he does not . . ." *Even if God doesn't rescue us from this, we still say no.*

I hope I always have the courage to say, "I know what God *can* do, but even if He doesn't, I still won't worship idols. I will still worship the one true God."

I know God can heal my friend's illness, but even if He doesn't . . .

I know God can fix relationships, but even if He doesn't . . .

I know God can provide a spouse, but even if He doesn't . . .

I know God can provide for me financially, but even if He doesn't . . .

Right? Even. If. He. Doesn't.

These three said it, knowing their lives were on the line, and they never looked back.

A lot of courageous noes make for some beautifully brave yeses.

They were brave. They said no. And even when the voices of fear must have been whispering to them, they didn't listen. They stood there in their no and believed that God is still God.

A lot of courageous noes make for some beautifully brave yeses.

And I'm not sure you are going to get it right every time—saying the right yeses and the right noes. I don't get it right all the time. But courage doesn't equal right; courage equals stepping out and trying.

Be brave and say yes. But also be brave and say no. Jump on the float. Walk into the furnace. Stand up. Sit down. Get on that flight. Say the thing that courage asks you to say, even if it's the word *no*.

Be Brave: *What's one thing you can say no to today that will make space for some better yeses in the future?*

Day Fifty-Six

>>>>——————

IN THE WAITING SEASON

Wait for the LORD; be strong, and let your heart take courage; wait for the LORD!

—PSALM 27:14 ESV

I wanted to fly back to Nashville from Dallas a day earlier than I had planned. I was tired of being on the road and had my plans change suddenly in Dallas, which meant I could go home twenty-four hours earlier than I thought.

So I jumped on the phone as soon as I realized I could go home. And after answering all the automated questions, I sat there on hold. For a long time. But I really wanted to go home, so I didn't hang up, though I seriously kept considering it.

It's just the unknown of waiting, you know? In those moments, I never know when to hang up. I could be the *very next caller* they speak with, or it could be another half hour. And then I think, *If I sit here, will they get to me soon? Or if I hang up and call back, will I somehow skip over the line of other customers on hold and immediately get to speak to a customer care representative?*

I almost wanted to cry because I feel like I'm waiting *everywhere*

Be brave enough to be patient—not just outwardly, but inwardly.

right now. On the phone, and in my life, I may be next in line, or maybe I'm not.

Are you in the waiting season right now? What do you do when you've said yes or you've said no, but you're still waiting? Where do you go from there?

Life is full of waiting seasons, and you can brave out the wait and do it well. Be brave enough to be patient—not just outwardly, but inwardly.

Jesus showed us this in His own life, and in today's scripture. He is compassionate, gracious, patient.

When we remember how patient the Lord is with us, it can help us be patient in our seasons of waiting. Waiting for our work to pay off. Waiting for a relationship to heal. Waiting for a trial to end.

You can be brave in whatever type of waiting season you find yourself when you are living in total dependence on your ever-patient, ever-present Father.

Be Brave: *Where are you waiting in your life right now? Write about it here or in your journal.*

Day Fifty-Seven

WHEN YOU HOLD ON

These hard times are small potatoes compared to the coming good times, the lavish celebration prepared for us. There's far more here than meets the eye. The things we see now are here today, gone tomorrow. But the things we can't see now will last forever.

—2 Corinthians 4:17–18 MSG

Amy Stroup sings a song called "Hold Onto Hope Love." It's been my companion more nights than I can count as I've cried to God about the rough patches on my hands from holding tightly to the cliff of hope when it would be easier to just let go and fall into hopelessness.

And the truth? It would be easier to let go. But it wouldn't be brave. It's just not the story God is writing with my life. It's not the story God is writing with yours either. So please, hold on.

Don't let go because it hurts or because it is hard. Don't let go because you feel like it is ridiculous to hold on. It's not. Hold on.

My friend dreams of adopting, and yet multiple babies come into her family's life only to go home with the birth mom. But my friend holds on. Christy is tired of running miles and miles every day, but she wants to run a marathon, so she doesn't quit. She holds on. Mike and his wife run a camp for students where the buildings get run-down, the staff turns over, and the pool always smells a little off (just a little). It gets hard to have their jobs. But they see Jesus show up for students every week during the summer, so they hold on.

Don't give up on life. Don't give up on God. Don't give up on yourself.

I hate it when people say, "God will never give us more than we can handle," mainly because I don't think it's true and it isn't in the Bible. The Bible does say no temptation will come to us that we cannot endure (1 Corinthians 10:13). You and I just have to be brave enough to hold on, even when our struggles feel like more than our hands can handle.

How long? I think the answer is to hold on until the Lord makes it really clear that you're supposed to let go. Ask God. Ask people you trust. Ask your own heart. But while you are listening, persevere, and lean toward holding on until God and other people make it really clear that you're supposed to let go.

Don't give up on life. Don't give up on God. Don't give up on yourself. Hold on to hope, love.

BE BRAVE: *Tell someone you trust how you are trying to hold on. Let someone encourage you. (And maybe listen to Amy Stroup's song. I think you'll love it.)*

Day Fifty-Eight

WHEN YOU LET GO

"Forget the former things; do not dwell on the past. See, I am doing a new thing! Now it springs up; do you not perceive it?"

—ISAIAH 43:18–19 NIV

Letting go has always been hard for me. Yet I have seen, over and over again, that to simply let go is a powerful catalyst God will use to move me toward the next best thing.

I couldn't grab hold of Nashville until I let go of Marietta.

I couldn't grab hold of Scotland until I let go of Nashville.

It's a wee bit easier to let go when you know what you are grabbing hold of. The monkey bar option, I like to call it. You are willing to let go of the current monkey bar because you can see the next one you want to grab.

(I have to be honest here. I have no arm strength. So monkey bars are about 0 percent fun for me. But I do know and understand how they work.)

The deeper call for courage comes when you let go with nothing ahead to grab.

Letting go like that is the hardest. That's when courage has to bubble out of you. That's when your insides have to be like steel. And all the times when God has been right before, in the Bible and in your life, play like a movie reel through your mind, reminding you of His faithfulness.

I have seen, over and over again, that to simply let go is a powerful catalyst God will use to move me toward the next best thing.

Sometimes you have to let go of things that are bad for you—addictions, abusive relationships, sinful habits. That takes courage too. It doesn't matter if the thing is good for you or bad for you—if it isn't the *best* for you, you have to let go.

It may be a relationship or a job or a city or some money or old hurts. When it is time to let go, you know it. Your fingers long to ease their grip, but your heart begs them to hold on—not because it's the best for you, but because the unknown is scary. Only in letting go are your hands free to grab on to the next thing.

Please let go. Please be brave enough to empty your hands without seeing the next monkey bar. You can trust in God even when you can't see the future—because He can!

I don't know what that looks like for you, so I can't write the exact words you need to hear. But I do know that courageous sacrifices are always worth it. So, friend, let go.

BE BRAVE: *Bob Goff says quit something every Thursday. What can you quit this week?*

Day Fifty-Nine

>>>>———

WHEN CHANGE HURTS

And we know that in all things God works for the good of
those who love him, who have been called according to his
purpose.

—ROMANS 8:28 NIV

've gone through a lot of changes in my life. Geographical
changes. Career changes. Relationship changes. And I'm someone who isn't the biggest fan of change. It's really just not my
favorite . . . as you have probably gathered by now.

And, friend, they are still happening! Just when I think life is
smooth sailing, here comes another change.

Listen. If you've learned nothing from this little section of the
book, and if I've learned nothing from simply living through all
the changes, let's all hear this—brave people are okay with change
because they remember that change is for our good.

That doesn't mean you have to love change or seek change or
want change. That doesn't mean that when something that seemed
to be going awesome takes an unexpected turn, you have to throw
a party. It means that if you're brave, you can walk through change

with grace and hope that God's promises are true and all things really do work together for good.

Some changes are welcomed. They're celebrated. They're fun. Promotions! Pregnancies! Book deals! Engagements! New homes! Though even the good changes in life can be difficult or stressful.

But then there are those other changes. The bad ones. The ones that don't seem to have any silver lining.

Often change hurts. Often change is painful. Devastating even.

Maybe you just lost your job and you're bracing yourself for the conversation you'll have with your spouse tonight. Maybe the results from your MRI came back, and normal, as you knew it, ends today.

Brave people are okay with change because they remember that change is for our good.

Just remember—a brave person's joy isn't dependent on circumstances. God has got this, whatever it is. Your family. Your career. Your relationships. He knows your pain. He cares about your pain. And He wants you to live bravely, in the strength and knowledge that He is working for your good and He is ultimately in control.

BE BRAVE: *You know what I hope after these few days talking about change together? I hope change just becomes this thing you plan for, you make space for in your life, and you choose to be brave about.*

BRAVE ENOUGH
TO PERSEVERE

Sometimes everything hurts.
Even when you are brave.

Day Sixty

LIFE IS HARD

"I have told you these things, so that in me you may have peace. In this world you will have trouble. But take heart! I have overcome the world!"

—JOHN 16:33 NIV

You don't need me to tell you this, do you? Life is hard.

I don't know what I thought I was signing up for, but I guess I thought things would be easier than this. Maybe I'm the slowest learner on our planet, but I'm still surprised every time a tragedy happens in my life or a situation takes a turn I didn't expect.

I landed in Texas a few weeks ago and turned my phone off of airplane mode. While I'm flying, all phone business halts, but the minute the wheels are down, I am back in action. I'm always excited to see what texts have come in while I was in the air, usually two or three, or if I'm lucky, five.

This day—*seventy-nine.* Between Nashville and Dallas, something had happened. The screen of my phone exploded with a waterfall of text messages. I couldn't even try to keep up as they blazed down my screen. But one word kept catching my eye.

DEAD

Someone was dead. I couldn't tell who; the messages were passing my eyes too quickly. But panic rose in my chest because I knew tragedy had just landed with me in Texas.

The next few hours were filled with grief and weeping and changing flights and booking flights and moments of not knowing what to do.

The nature of tragedy, huh? It sneaks up on you and sends your world into a tailspin, and then it is weeks, months, years of questions and pain and sadness and grief.

You can be sad. You can be angry. You can be confused. But you don't ever have reason to despair.

I felt it in the death of someone I loved. I felt it when my pastor stood on our church's stage and said he was leaving. I felt it when the text came through that said our relationship was done. (*Over text?* I know. The worst.)

Life isn't always easy. In fact, I think I'm growing to believe that life isn't often easy. My friend Mike Foster, founder of People of the Second Chance, said it this way on Twitter, and I love it so much I want to tattoo it on my arm:

> *"Life is messy, hard, and weird. We don't need to act surprised anymore."*

Right? So simple and yet brilliant. And so important to remember. (Hence the tattoo idea.)

God knows that life is painful.

So, yeah, you can be sad. You can be angry. You can be confused. But you don't ever have reason to despair. Even when it gets tragic and dark, do not despair. You are braver than that.

Be Brave: *I don't know what kinds of hurt or tragedy you are facing right now, but I know, as Mike said, life is messy, hard, and weird. Allow yourself to feel that today.*

Day Sixty-One

>>>>

FAILURE IS INEVITABLE

See what kind of love the Father has given to us, that we
should be called children of God; and so we are.

—1 JOHN 3:1 ESV

I f you think I'm funny, (1) thanks and (2) thank my dad. Dad is a
lot of things, including very, very funny. We talk on the phone
a lot, and we often share jokes back and forth. For example, if I
tell my friends a story at dinner and they laugh a lot, I will almost
always call my dad the next day and tell him the story, including
describing the reaction from the others at the table. (And probably
what we ate too. We are a family of foodies.)

Often, as we are hanging up, my dad will say, "Who loves ya?"—
and then, before I even have time to answer, he says, "Dada. Dada."

Now, mind you, none of us have called him "Dada" in approximately twenty years, but it still works.

Why do I like that so much?

I think it's really nice when other people remind you that you are
loved. I walk through every day, winning or losing, with that truth
in mind.

It makes me brave.

When you know who loves you, you know your safe places. You know where you can rest. You know where you can go when you fail. (I'm sorry if I'm the first to tell you this, but brave or not, you *are* going to fail.)

Failing doesn't make you a failure. Trying something new makes you brave.

It's when we let it define us that things go wrong.

Brave people don't let failure define them; they let failure teach them.

> *Failing doesn't make you a failure. Trying something new makes you brave.*

Brave people know that because they are loved by their heavenly Father, they can fail and fail and fail again, and nothing between them and their Father will change. Literally. Nothing.

Brave people have courage because they know God loves them no matter what.

Be Brave: *I keep a dry-erase marker in my bathroom so I can write notes on my mirror. Grab one for yourself, and write on your mirror, "I am deeply loved by God." Leave it there for one week and see how it impacts your heart.*

Day Sixty-Two

>>>>———

DON'T BE AFRAID

"Have I not commanded you? Be strong and courageous.
Do not be afraid; do not be discouraged, for the LORD your
God will be with you wherever you go."

—JOSHUA 1:9 NIV

*P*lease don't let fear win.

Being brave looks different for each person because each person has a unique call from God.

What is the big question lingering in your heart that you don't know how to answer? Is it a question you're too afraid to answer? It could be big, like a location change, a job change, or a relationship.

Should you pick up and move?

Should you change career paths even though you're well into your fifties?

Should you pursue something romantic with that person you've been "just friends" with for ten years?

If the reason you don't say yes to any of those questions is simply, "I'm afraid," then you need to seek the Lord and ask Him to help you be brave, and then answer those questions based on what He leads you to do.

Connor didn't know when he said yes to playing baseball in his senior year at Vanderbilt (instead of going to the major leagues when he was drafted as a junior) that he would have his best year on the field and off in Nashville, thus earning him a higher draft spot after his senior season.

Please don't let fear win.

Ashley didn't know when she said yes to moving to Kansas City to be an intern at the International House of Prayer that the man who would become her husband had done the same.

I didn't know when I went on that first trip to Scotland that my life would forever be tied to that country and the people there.

Friend, we can't see the future, so when we take steps forward, we've got to say no to fear.

God wants you to be "strong and courageous." Why? Because He's got this! Your life. Your plan. Your future.

God cares about it, and He's with you. He's with me. He's with *us*.

Be Brave: *Where are you letting fear hold you back?*

Day Sixty-Three

FACE YOUR PAIN

Even though I walk through the valley of the shadow of death, I will fear no evil, for you are with me; your rod and your staff, they comfort me.

—PSALM 23:4 ESV

It's been many a year that I have wrestled and worked through how to deal with the lies in my head about how God made me and who I am and how I look. It's always been a big deal to me.

But that doesn't mean I don't still struggle. I'm an Enneagram Type Seven—I want to run from my pain. It's my natural tendency. Fight or flight, and I will spread my wings.

The lies still come. Sometimes they are a whisper when I am walking onto a stage, sometimes they are a quick cut when I see a picture of myself, and other times, they scream. They scream in a way I cannot describe—they are constant and vulgar and violently unkind.

And when the lies get loud like that in my head—the ones that say I am painfully ugly, ruined, unsalvageable, disappointing, and so forth—the first step, I have learned, is to invite truth in. So I stand there, or sit there, or lie there, and I say the true things.

God made me on purpose.

God loves me unconditionally.

God doesn't make ugly.

Bible verses long memorized about who I am, how I was made perfectly, and how God treasures me.

And repeat, repeat, repeat.

When someone else knows, it's better.

I told my counselor this week—I spoke the lies to her, the ones that have screamed at me recently. I told her where I heard them and who was there and what I was wearing and way more detail than she could ever want. When someone else knows, it's better.

It's better because when you say the thing out loud, you're facing it. And that's brave. Telling someone about your pain—whether it's lies the enemy plants in your head or a devastating circumstance you're wading through—is brave.

When you face the pain—look at it and call it what it is—you will begin to experience healing. Pushing the pain down or trying to ignore it? That's not brave. That's not healthy. And hiding it doesn't lead to healing.

Face your pain. Bring it to God. Bring it to your counselor. Bring it to another person and find healing there.

Be Brave: *Friend, are you hurting? Don't run from it anymore.*

Day Sixty-Four

>>>>———

INVITE SOMEONE
INTO YOUR PAIN

You can't whitewash your sins and get by with it; you find
mercy by admitting and leaving them.

—Proverbs 28:13 msg

I remember being in eighth grade and getting a phone call from
my friend Brittany. "Annie," she said, "I think I've figured out a
way for us to lose weight before the dance in May." I was all ears.
"We'll just take these pills that make you have diarrhea." And so for
about a week, I did. Let me tell you, there is no more horrible experience. Did I lose weight? Barely. I felt horrible, my hair lost its shine,
and my stomach was upset the entire time.

I have known so many people who have struggled with eating
disorders. It is such a painful cycle. And it feels like such a shameful
thing that the person struggling with it becomes secretive. And the
one suffering hides his or her pain.

Also, people caught up in any sort of secret sin get defensive,
elusive, and sad. It is just like with a sore or injury—if you hide it, it

festers (ew). If you show a doctor, you will be on the road to recovery.

Don't keep secrets.

Tell somebody you trust. Please. The darkness can't hang around when it's exposed in the light.

You may need a counselor or a pastor, or you can invite friends in, but it needs to be someone with more authority in your life than just a friend.

Proverbs 28:13 is the real deal. It's God's Word. Sin and pain thrive in the darkness. They love a good secret. And, friend, I know it—you've got to be brave to tell that shameful thing to those people you want to like you.

Darkness can't hang around when it's exposed in the light.

But just try it, and you'll be surprised. You'll be surprised how often people give grace. You'll be surprised at how quickly the light eliminates the darkness, and despite what your mind tells you, you will feel braver once it's out in the open.

BE BRAVE: *Friend, tell someone you trust what pain you are experiencing. Don't keep secrets anymore.*

Day Sixty-Five

>>>———

DIVINE DETOURS

Many are the plans in a person's heart, but it is the LORD's purpose that prevails.

—PROVERBS 19:21 NIV

You know that thing where you think your life is going one way and then something changes? You may be like, *Wait a minute. I thought I was going to be a nurse. Why did I* not *get into that nursing school?*

My standout divine detour happened when I applied to get into the school of education at the University of Georgia. Remember how I told you that being a teacher was my lifelong dream?

Well, I applied to the school of education. And . . . I didn't get in the first time. To be fair, I had kind of slacked in the first two years of college, but I mean, my grades weren't *bad*. But when I didn't get in, I thought, *I have always wanted to be a teacher. What do I do?*

And it broke my heart because I had never planned for a different career.

So I ended up having to explore other things for a couple of months and thinking, *Okay, my life plan has changed . . .*

And that was a divine detour I had to work through. It was so good for me to walk through that, even the painful parts.

After a few months, a spot came open in the program, and they let me in, so I got to pursue teaching after all.

But the Lord has given me divine detours like that more than once, where I've had to work through the question—*What if I don't actually get to do the thing I want to do?*

Divine detours are no fun in the moment. Whether they involve work, dating, friendships, church, or family, they're a shock. They're a change in plan that you didn't ask for.

But the thing is, we need divine detours because it's through the divine detours that God always takes us where we're supposed to go in the long run.

God is God, and He loves you, so oftentimes a divine detour may just be His way of getting you to look up at Him and be brave enough to ask the hardest of hard questions, like, *God . . . do I trust You, even if I don't understand what You're doing?*

> *What if I don't actually get to do the thing I want to do?*

God sees the whole picture. Your whole story. Your future. You can trust Him, even when He derails your plan, because He is good and He loves you.

Be Brave: *In your journal, list two or three divine detours that have happened in your life. As you look back now, can you see how they worked out for your good in the end?*

Day Sixty-Six

WHY PERSEVERANCE MATTERS

Not only so, but we also glory in our sufferings, because we know that suffering produces perseverance; perseverance, character; and character, hope. And hope does not put us to shame, because God's love has been poured out into our hearts through the Holy Spirit, who has been given to us.

—ROMANS 5:3–5 NIV

I'm a quitter. It comes way too easy for me to walk away from something that feels hard, whether it's an exercise class, a friendship, or a diet. But as I mature and grow up, I'm learning that courage builds when I persevere.

Listen. I've wanted to walk away from this career a lot. And I mean *a lot*. It gets hard and lonely and frustrating (along with all the good things—don't get me wrong!). But I'm hanging on because I see the light at my feet telling me to keep walking and writing.

Joy Williams has a song called "Golden Thread," and when things seem to be stretching me too thin, I loop that song like nobody's business. It reminds me that when I feel like I am just hanging by a thread and everything seems to be unraveling and to simply cut it would be the best bet, that thread may be gold. And it may be worth holding on.

Perseverance builds character.

Things can get sticky here. You're in an abusive relationship? I'm not telling you to stay and persevere. You're trying to make it as an actress in LA and you're literally out of money? I'm not telling you to stay and persevere.

If you're tired of fighting for that prayer that never seems to be answered? Hold on. Persevere. Because perseverance builds character. And God does answer prayer.

If you want to walk away from your marriage to a godly man because it has become something different than you thought it'd be? Hold on. Persevere. (Get counseling, but persevere.)

If you have applied to the college of your dreams but haven't heard back yet? Hold on. Persevere.

I got a tattoo on my right arm that says just that. *Persevere.* In tiny white letters, it's there to remind me of who I want to be and how I want to live.

Brave people don't give up. Brave people don't quit. Brave people realize that we rejoice in our sufferings because it leads to perseverance and perseverance produces character, and ultimately, it brings us to the hope we have in Jesus. Hope is worth fighting for.

Be Brave: *What does perseverance look like for you today?*

Day Sixty-Seven

DON'T GIVE UP

Let us not become weary in doing good, for at the proper
time we will reap a harvest if we do not give up.

—GALATIANS 6:9 NIV

Look at you! I'm impressed. Look how far you've gotten in this
book. Listen. You're on Day 67! Amazing. You are showing perseverance already.

Okay, I'm going to tell you something, and I want you to listen.
Don't give up. Don't quit! You're on a journey. You're looking for
brave. You're over halfway through what God has for you here.

You've been looking at your life—at your pain and joys and
calling—and you've been finding the brave. But don't quit now.
Don't quit trying to find the brave in your life. Don't quit the things
you're involved in that feel *just too hard.* Don't quit this book.

Looking for brave and doing things
that are healthy for your mind, body, and
soul will reap a harvest of blessing.

You know when you're working out
and you start seeing some results? You're

*Don't quit! You're
on a journey.*

stronger, you feel better, and your clothes fit a little better. And then you're like, "I'm done!" And you abandon all healthy habits.

Don't do that with your soul (or your healthy habits either).

If you stick with this—if you stick with spending time in God's Word, journaling and looking inward and holding your choices up against Scripture—you will reap a harvest of blessing.

Don't quit believing that, and don't give up now!

BE BRAVE: *Go on a short walk today. Think through the first two-thirds of this book and how you have changed because you have persevered and walked toward courage.*

Day Sixty-Eight

>>>> ——————

WHEN PAIN HEALS

On hearing this, Jesus said, "It is not the healthy who need a doctor, but the sick."

—MATTHEW 9:12 NIV

I got LASIK eye surgery recently. It's amazing. It feels like the closest thing to a miracle that I have ever experienced—I was blind but now I can see!

But it didn't feel great. There was a lot of pressure and a decent amount of pain that afternoon after the surgery. But I know the pain was worth it because now my eyesight is practically perfect.

Surgery hurts, but it is always for our good and for our health.

There are times when God is going to take you through surgery, not because He wants to hurt you, but because He loves you and wants to heal you. I've seen it in my own life—things being cut away, sins being revealed, secrets being exposed, all for my good. Even when it hurt.

We know that, and yet we often behave like our Surgeon isn't trustworthy and isn't out for our good. We live our lives panicking and worrying and wondering why our lives are full of pain.

There are times when God's going to take you through surgery, not because He wants to hurt you, but because He wants to heal you.

When we remember we're sinners in need of Jesus, we can trust our Great Physician. Jesus reminded us that we are sick people who need a doctor.

We cannot see the future. We do not know what's best for us. We make mistakes. We say things we regret. We do things with impure motives. We live in a broken world.

But our God is a Healer. He loves us. And we can be brave in the face of brokenness and pain and spiritual surgery because we know that God is good.

BE BRAVE: *Ask God to show you how some of your hurts have actually led to healing.*

Brave Enough to Pursue Healing

Healing is often a choice.

Day Sixty-Nine

>>>———→

GOD'S PURPOSE
FOR YOUR BODY

Or do you not know that your body is a temple of the Holy Spirit
within you, whom you have from God? You are not your own.

—1 Corinthians 6:19 esv

I weigh more than most women my age. I don't like talking about it.
It has been a fact since the fourth grade, it's something I struggle
with pretty much every day, and if I talk about it, it makes it more
real or a bigger deal or something.

I've been on a diet, or wanting to be on a diet, since I was in the
sixth grade. For those of you who keep calculations at home, that is
more than two-thirds of my life.

When I was in my early twenties, I was diagnosed with polycys-
tic ovary syndrome (PCOS). Among some other lovely side effects,
PCOS makes it difficult to lose weight and process insulin.

I spent most of my adolescent years thinking that because I was
treating my body badly, it didn't work right in many areas. But it
turns out that I had a disease working against me as well.

When I was a teenager, I was very focused on my body and my wants and needs, but my soul? Not as much. Speaking of my soul, I thought food fed it. The places that felt empty in me, I filled with food. Lonely? Eat. Sad? Eat. Celebrate? Eat.

Being diagnosed with PCOS felt like a light at the end of the tunnel. *So* this *is why I can't get skinny*, I thought, *and* this *is why I hate my body.*

It has taken years, and it's still a struggle—but by God's grace, I've gone from thinking my body is never good enough to believing it's a temple of the Holy Spirit.

God has a purpose for your body— with all its imperfections and sicknesses.

I pursue healing for my PCOS, and you may have a lifelong condition you wish would disappear too, but remember: Jesus makes all things new. One day our bodies and this broken world will be totally healed. In the meantime, God has a purpose for your body—with all its imperfections and sicknesses. He wants to use you, as you are, to bring glory to Himself.

Brave people look at the bodies they are in and choose to see them for what they are—vessels that hold a mighty God.

BE BRAVE: *We are going all in for the next few days on your health. Why? Because only a working body can be a brave body. We have spent time talking about our minds and our spirits, so prepare your heart as we dive into talking about our bodies.*

Day Seventy

RHYTHMS OF DISCIPLINE

For the moment all discipline seems painful rather than pleasant, but later it yields the peaceful fruit of righteousness to those who have been trained by it.

—Hebrews 12:11 esv

I decided to run a half marathon one spring several years ago. It was a ridiculous decision. I don't like running.

I signed up, paid my money, and booked my flight to Florida and was immediately full of regret. But the other girls doing it with me—Blair, Katie, and Emily—had signed up, paid, and booked as well, so there was no backing out.

I downloaded a training program to my iPhone the fall before the race and decided I would spend six months really training for this half marathon.

I didn't.

So by the time March rolled around and we were packing for the weekend, I had jogged approximately three miles in my training.

And I was about to attempt thirteen. And one-tenth.

After more than three and a half hours, I crossed that finish line. Only three gift packs remained on the table, and in the official standings of thousands of racers, I finished next to last.

Three grandmas walking finished in front of me.

The next week was the most painful week of my life. Every muscle hurt. Every. Single. One. I walked like I had just ridden a horse from Maine to that very Florida beach. I pretty much just wanted to lie on the floor like a starfish, with an IV of ibuprofen for two or ten days.

Discipline is the work done on the practice field so you are ready for the big game.

My lack of training—and lack of discipline—really came back to haunt me after that race.

I could have done better in that race, dealt with less pain, and possibly been willing to attempt another race of that distance had I actually trained.

Discipline has always felt like rules to me, and even though I'm a natural-born rule follower, when I'm the one making the rules and trying to keep them, it's not as natural. The truth is that discipline isn't rules you have to live by or laws you have to obey. Discipline is the work done on the practice field so you are ready for the big game.

What does that discipline look like? I don't know for you. I just know that I often like to label discipline as something boring and unnecessary when really, if you want to be brave and be ready to be called into the game, you have to practice.

Your discipline, the rhythm that makes you the best you—whether it's training your body, your mind, or your spirit—shows up when it is time to say the right thing, do the right thing, be the brave person you want to be. It's the practice that makes perfect, and the practice that makes you brave.

Be Brave: *What's one area of your life where you could be more disciplined?*

Day Seventy-One

PLEASE PLAY

This is the day that the LORD has made; let us rejoice and
be glad in it.

—PSALM 118:24 ESV

Yesterday—discipline. Today—let's play. Yes. Play! The two go
hand in hand more than you may realize. Do you have fun in
your daily life?

It may not seem important or brave to make play a priority, but
you have got to be brave to step away from responsibilities. To dis-
miss the lie that your career will fall apart if you spend some time
having fun.

Play outside. Play with your friends. Do the things you loved to
do when you were a kid because it reconnects you to a simpler time,
stress wasn't quite such a thing, and your heart was a simpler place
to live and love.

It's almost like a deep breath on a really hard journey of courage.

I was on a mission trip in Scotland, and our whole team was
arguing. Some things had gone wrong, and we had just been in tight
quarters for too long. So our team leaders canceled a three-hour

It's almost like a deep breath on a really hard journey of courage.

afternoon we had planned and instead took our team to go play Ultimate Frisbee.

People were slamming into each other and running and jumping and flying through the air. It was really aggressive, and we started out mad.

But do you know what happened? We ended up laughing.

It was a great example of how play can heal and how play matters to us and why we've got to do that. Being disciplined and being brave are not easy tasks. If you don't make space in your life for play, you will burn out. You will be in that spot where you are fighting for brave because you are feeling failure well up and fears arrive uninvited and there will be no healthy release. So play.

Brave people know that it's not just okay to play. It's healthy.

This day that you're in? This is the day the Lord has made. You can rejoice and be glad in it. You can have fun and laugh and be peaceful about your to-do list because God is in control, and you can have total peace in Him.

BE BRAVE: *Go play! For real, do something fun.*

Day Seventy-Two

>>>———

PLEASE EXERCISE

I appeal to you therefore, brothers, by the mercies of God, to present your bodies as a living sacrifice, holy and acceptable to God, which is your spiritual worship.

—ROMANS 12:1 ESV

Here's the thing. Yes, exercise. But not just to look good. Sure, exercise makes you look and feel healthier, but that's not why you should do it. A lifestyle of daily exercise is not about losing weight.

Your size isn't the issue. There isn't an attractive size or an ugly size. But there is a point at which you become unhealthy and your body suffers.

Exercise doesn't have to consist of running a marathon, unless that's something you want to do. (I have no clue why that would be "fun," but if it makes you happy, go for it.) Just go on a walk. Join a gym or a recreational sports team. Just get out there and move your body.

Your body needs to be honored and treated well. Your body was meant to move; it was not meant to be still.

You need your muscles and your bones to be strong enough to

do all the things you were called to do for as many years as you're meant to be here.

In Romans, Paul told us to present our bodies as a living sacrifice, and here is the truth of the matter: if we don't take care of our bodies, we are limiting our ability to do His work. Seriously. If we aren't kind to our bodies, if we aren't treating our bodies well, we are shortening our impact on the planet. I really believe that.

Your body was meant to move; it was not meant to be still.

God has put us on this planet to spread His love, to be His love to the people around us, and He's given us these amazing bodies to get us from point A to point B.

You know what's not brave? Being a couch potato. Taking care of your body and being strong so you can help others? *That* is brave. Brave people exercise and see it as a form of obedience to God.

You can do this, friend. I believe in you. You can stop viewing your body as a thing you want to be smaller or bigger or this or that and start viewing it as a temple of God that you get to spend your life caring for and using for His glory.

Be Brave: *Take a walk. Go to the gym. Go swimming. Train for a 5K. As my yoga studio sign always says, pursue sweat.*

Day Seventy-Three

PLEASE EAT YOUR VEGGIES

So, whether you eat or drink, or whatever you do, do all to
the glory of God.

—1 Corinthians 10:31 esv

I have a deep love for all things ice cream (well, almond milk ice
cream because I have a dairy allergy). Mix it with chocolate-chip
cookie dough, and I'm on cloud nine. But I can't eat ice cream for
breakfast, lunch, and dinner. Not for a lack of skill or desire—I have
the determination and the want to pull that off.

I know it isn't healthy for my body, and so I choose to eat it
maybe once a week or once a month. Moderation is key, friends.
Moderation. And prayer. Weird? Maybe. But trust me that when
you sit down and ask the Lord to direct how you eat, He will.

I have grown to love my body, to love the way God made me, so
I can't imagine filling my body with food or drink that will destroy
it. I try to choose the things that will represent the Lord well.

What are you feeding yourself?

I understand that we all have differing resources. Some people can afford to have fresh fruit and veggies delivered to their doorstep. For others, paying the grocery bill is a struggle. I get that.

But here's the thing. No matter what your socioeconomic status is, you should be thinking about what you're eating, not just inhaling.

If McDonald's is where you're eating today, there's a side salad for about the same price as a burger.

I'm not saying you can never eat the burger. Burgers are fantastic, but if you thoughtlessly consume food that tastes good and fail to consume food that is actually good for you, you are not treating your body well.

God has given your body to you for a reason. He has a purpose for your life. Be brave enough to make your eating habits intentional.

You should be thinking about what you're eating, not just inhaling.

God doesn't want one compartment of your life to honor Him. He wants your everything. He wants every part of you and your identity to bring glory to Him.

We've got to be thoughtful. We've got to take care of this gift that is our body.

BE BRAVE: *Let me tell you what you need to do. Go to a farmers' market today. Even if you don't know what to buy, just find your local farmers' market and walk through it. See the colors and the seasonal offers. Notice the farmers and ask them questions. Buy one vegetable, one that you know you can google how to cook, and try it!*

Day Seventy-Four

>>>>—————

PLEASE REST

It's useless to rise early and go to bed late, and work your worried fingers to the bone. Don't you know he enjoys giving rest to those he loves?

—Psalm 127:2 msg

B rave people recognize that there are times when you have to stop.

Listen, I'm all about the hustle. You've got to work. You've got to exercise. You've got to say yes. You've got to try. You've got to work hard, my friend. For sure.

But hustling for 365 days is not what brave people do. They stop when they need to stop, even if it's scary and a little bit costly.

Your spiritual health is more important than that goal you're hustling toward. And you won't meet your goals if you burn out.

Rest is not a bad thing. Rest is not something that will make you fall behind. But yes, it may be costly sometimes. Sometimes you will have to say no to something so you can rest.

But just like today's verse says, God gives rest to His beloved. Friend, bravery isn't conquering the world in your own strength. It's working hard with what you're given, but also trusting that everything comes from God—your ability to hustle is from God. He created You.

So listen to Him when He tells you to rest. Make rest a rhythmic part of your life. It is a discipline you have to choose and invite into your life. When you see others hustling around you and forsaking rest, don't get antsy and feel like you have to keep up.

You won't meet your goals if you burn out.

Be brave enough to rest—knowing that you need it. Knowing that it's healthy. Knowing that even God Himself rests.

BE BRAVE: *Take a nap. Go to bed early tonight. Take a day off from work (or even just an afternoon). Find rest.*

Day Seventy-Five

>>> ———

SABBATH

"Do your work in six days and rest on the seventh day."
—Exodus 34:21 CEV

*B*rave people take a Sabbath. It doesn't have to look the way it looks in Jerusalem. You don't have to avoid using a light switch from sundown to sundown, but you've got to take time away from the grind. Regularly.

For me, my Sabbath is Wednesday mornings (since I often work on weekends).

So Wednesdays, from when I wake up until two or three in the afternoon, I'm not available. Everybody knows it. What that means is that I have a six-hour window when I don't use technology and I don't do laundry and I don't hustle.

The only things I do are rest and worship.

If it's restful for me to get coffee with a friend, I get coffee with a friend.

If it's restful for me to admire God's creation at Radnor Lake, I go walk at Radnor Lake.

I read books. I read like crazy. I just read until I'm tired of reading. And then I always take a nap. Sometimes I drive down to Leiper's Fork, Tennessee, about thirty minutes from my house, and just lay out a blanket and read for a bit there. And yes, maybe I nap there too.

It is really hard to take a day off of work, or some hours away, when I know there is a lot to be done.

It sounds awesome, and it is, but it is also really hard to take a day off of work, or some hours away, when I know there is a lot to be done.

It takes courage to walk away from your job or your calling for a bit, believing that God will still provide. But Sabbath is something we are called to—a discipline that will make our lives better if we embrace it.

Friend, you and I? We can't let the fear of missing out (or FOMO, as the kids call it these days) on an amazing opportunity to win.

We need Sabbath. We need rest. We need people. We need friendship.

Brave friends, please choose to have a Sabbath. Unplug. Give yourself a break. Say yes to rest and yes to relationships, even if you're saying, "Hold on a sec" to your job or your calling.

Be Brave: *Grab the book* Garden City *by John Mark Comer. It's a great read and has really helpful information about Sabbath.*

Day Seventy-Six

WORDS CAN HEAL

The words of the reckless pierce like swords, but the tongue
of the wise brings healing.

—PROVERBS 12:18 NIV

We have two options when we use our words: we can build or
we can destroy.

I could tell you story after story of how someone's words
gave me life, built me up, strengthened me, brought healing. And I
can tell you stories of how words have broken my heart.

They. Are. Powerful.

I know this because I've felt it over and over. But this one time
in seventh grade left a defining mark on my heart. Words changed
me forever.

That year my social studies teacher was Mr. Samson. His classroom had lots of windows, and the desks were squished together.
I sat between two boys and behind my best friend. I watched one
day as one of the boys borrowed a tiny green piece of paper from
my friend Sarah and began to make some sort of list. I don't know

how I knew, but I knew that list was about me. I couldn't see it, but watching him write told me everything. I was equal parts worried and curious.

Class ended. Mark ripped the green paper into tiny squares, and as he walked out of the classroom, he dropped them in the trash can. After the classroom cleared, I slowly packed up, and with Mr. Samson's eyes following my every move, I knelt down and scooped up those tiny squares from the trash and shoved them into the left front pocket of my acid-wash jeans. (The nineties, y'all.)

We have two options when we use our words: we can build or we can destroy.

I got home that afternoon, and after dinner I went upstairs to my room and spread those squares out across the carpeted floor. Like completing some type of evil puzzle, I mixed and matched pieces until the frayed edges met and the words began to come together. I taped the pieces as they lined up, and since the pieces were so small, the paper started to feel laminated with Scotch tape.

I began to read the text in that classic middle school dude, chicken-scratch handwriting. It was a list of every girl in our class with one word used to describe them.

I zeroed in on my own name. And my line looked like this:

Annie = Flabby

I know you've had words hurt you, like I have. Because if you are a human person, you have experienced the pain of words firsthand.

I know because I've been a human person my whole life. And

I've known a lot of human people. And I've talked to a lot of human people. And I've been mean to human people.

Look at today's verse. Reckless words? They hurt. But words can heal too. Brave people don't gossip and use their words to hurt others.

Brave people use their words to heal. Speaking with kindness about other people's hearts and minds *and* bodies can go a long way to heal. Brave people let God's Word and the words of the wise bring healing to their own hearts. May you see the healing, feel the healing, that comes from the tongue of the wise.

BE BRAVE: *Who could you speak to today to offer some healing?*

Day Seventy-Seven

HEALTHY PEOPLE THINK ABOUT OTHER PEOPLE

Jesus replied: "'Love the Lord your God with all your heart and with all your soul and with all your mind.' This is the first and greatest commandment. And the second is like it: 'Love your neighbor as yourself.' All the Law and the Prophets hang on these two commandments."

—MATTHEW 22:37–40 NIV

In high school my mind was full of evil whispers of how unlovely I was, how much I needed to change, and how God had messed up when He made me. I didn't know then that I could call those whispers "lies," so I let them fester and grow until they were kudzu covering my soul. And I lived like that, in self-hatred, for years.

Once during my sophomore year, my mom was taking me home from soccer practice and asked me a pointed question: "How do you think you can love your friends if you don't love yourself?"

I was puzzled. *Who cares if I love me?* I thought. I remember genuinely considering that my mother did not know what she was talking about.

(Shocking no mom ever—a teenager thought she knew best.)

She didn't push me; she just let me mull over her question in my mind. I don't know that I even answered her; if I did, it was something teen-angsty, like, "Uh, Mom, you don't even understand how much I love my friends and I love God and that's all that matters." And then I probably got out of the minivan and took my sweaty soccer self, sat on her beautiful couch, and waited for her to cook dinner for our family. (So what I'm saying is, I was a real pleasure as a teen.)

That conversation has stuck with me for all these years. And as I grew up, and God rescued me from many of those lies and taught me how to fight for truth, I realized (*gasp*) that my mother was right.

While we are capable of loving others to some degree even when we are drowning in self-hate, there is a freedom in love that comes with following the second greatest commandment.

To love someone is to believe in *them*. When someone believes in you, it changes everything—how you carry yourself, how you treat others, how you live day after day. You can give that same gift to those around you.

You have to love yourself to love others well.

My mom was right: you have to love yourself to love others well. Jesus said it Himself—love others *as* you love yourself. That's something worth thinking through.

If you're truly being brave and if you're truly pursuing health, you grow to love yourself and you love other people out of that.

Healthy, brave people love other people.

Do you love yourself? Do you see yourself the way God sees you? Do you recognize how absolutely lovable you are? Because when you do, when you see all that truth, you can't help loving your neighbor.

Be Brave: *Look back at the title of today—Healthy People Think About Other People—and it's because they love themselves first that they are able to love other people. Think about this and write about it today: Would your life and relationships look different if you lived that truth? That to love others is an overflow of God's love to you and your love for yourself?*

BRAVE ENOUGH
TO SERVE

Give who you are.
The world will be
a better place for it.

Day Seventy-Eight

>>>———

BE A MENTOR

Follow my example, as I follow the example of Christ.

—1 Corinthians 11:1 niv

A few years ago, I was hanging with two of the girls from my church small group, talking about college and dudes and the Lent season and gal stuff. We were discussing our plans for small group that night, and I mentioned, in passing, that the girls should bring their journals. To my utter shock, neither of them had a journal. It took me a minute to remember that they were not that much older than I was when I began journaling.

So that night, when the girls arrived and we finished eating our taco soup, I pulled the huge, clear plastic tub from the hallway closet and showed them my ever-growing collection of journals.

Every notebook I have written in, scribbled on, and cried over for the last twenty years is stored in this container. I pulled out specific ones and told the girls about my memories from that season of life. How the one with the photograph of a little boy and girl in black and white was from my freshman year of college, and I accidentally left it at church one day and felt panicked because I wrote about my crush in there. How the one with the hand-drawn armor of God went along on the first mission trip I led. And I showed them the first one, with the white and gold stars, not even halfway full, but so meaningful.

It was a sweet experience for them to see some of my history and for me to look back through some of those formative seasons of my life.

The Bible challenges men and women to lead by example and also to teach and pour into those younger than they are, a few steps behind. Mentoring high school and college students has brought me so much joy. It is life-giving to take what the Lord's taught you and pass it down to those who are right behind you in their walk of life.

The Bible challenges men and women to lead by example and also to teach and pour into those younger than they are, a few steps behind.

A common roadblock for people is that they feel unqualified. Who am I to mentor someone? If you're walking with Jesus, you have wisdom to pass down to those who haven't been walking with Him for as long as you have.

Brave people don't just pour into their own hopes and dreams. They pour their wisdom and time and love into others.

Be Brave: *Think of someone younger than you whom you could take to coffee this week. Give him or her a call and make time to hang out!*

Day Seventy-Nine

BLAZE A TRAIL

Your word is a lamp to my feet and a light to my path.

—Psalm 119:105 esv

A few years ago, I sat across the table in a coffee shop here in Nashville as a young single girl told me of her aches and pains and the faith issues that, in her mind, were directly related to her singleness. (I hear ya, sister.) She didn't cry, but I held a napkin in my grip because I thought for sure she would at any moment. She told me stories—many that I felt she was pulling from my own journal as a twentysomething single Christian gal—and I told her what I never knew to tell myself.

"I know. It hurts. But God has not forgotten you. He is showing you His love for you, even now. Believe Him. Believe His Word. Believe His heart."

I had just started writing publicly about my single life, and this girl had noticed. And she asked me, "Why now? What is it about this year that made you finally want to talk about it?"

"God," I said. "He just made it clear this was the right time."

Without hesitation, she said, "I'm so glad. We all need trailblazers. Now that I see that *you've* done this, I genuinely think I can do it too."

I almost laughed. Trailblazer? Sister, if this is trailblazing, I am the most cut-up, ill-equipped, whiny leader a team has ever encountered.

"Thy Word is a lamp unto my feet and a light unto my path," I sing in my head as the tears pour and I push forward on this trail. To be honest, I never meant for this to be my path, but can my pain make it easier for someone else?

You, my friend, married or single, female or male, you are blazing a trail with your life for the younger women and men behind you. They will have their own overgrowth to challenge them, and they will lead the way for others.

> "*We all need trailblazers. Now that I see that* you've *done this, I genuinely think I can do it too.*"

Because you are making a way for them, saving them some pain that your bloodied arms prove is real, and honoring their footsteps by providing a clear path.

You get the chance to live courageously. You were meant for it. You were born for it. It never feels easy, and it never is free. But it is what we want more than anything else.

Never forget as you step forward with your life that you are a trailblazer.

BE BRAVE: *Where are you trailblazing?*

Day Eighty

>>>>

EVERYTHING YOU
HAVE IS GOD'S

The earth and everything on it belong to the LORD. The world and its people belong to him.

—PSALM 24:1 CEV

We are born with a "Mine!" mentality. Our stuff, our money, our talents, our résumés, our status as humans . . . all of it shapes our identity.

But God gives us a new identity in Christ. Now we are His. We are stewards of His stuff. So your time, your money, all your resources, even your story—it's God's, my friend.

Living with that understanding takes courage because the natural thing is for us to want to claim everything—*mine, mine, mine!* We want credit for and control of the good things in our lives, and we want to decide how to live based on what we want.

Living for self? That's easy. Living like everything you have is God's (because it is)? That's brave.

I didn't write about my singleness for a long time. And honestly, often I still feel the pull to be silently single. It would be easier. I wouldn't have to tell some of the embarrassing or sad personal stories you've read throughout my books, many of them happening in the singleness that

Living for self? That's easy. Living like everything you have is God's (because it is)? That's brave.

I wear every day. But as much as I willingly surrendered to the voice of God that told me to use my story to encourage others, I know this is going to hurt sometimes. And I am not strong enough to write about this.

But I'm still typing. The truth is, I'm doing this through no strength of my own. Trust me. The inner Annie is crying uncle and begging me to stop and walk away and just. Give. Up.

It's God in me, gently asking me if I'm willing to be brave for you and share this story of mine, this story that belongs to Him, like I'm asking you to be brave for others.

If it is my time to talk about being single, then it is the time that will bring God the most glory and us the most good.

So what is it for you? Have you been too scared to share your testimony of redemption because you don't want your secret sins out there? Have you been too scared to give your resources away because you're afraid you won't have what you "need" to do what you want to do?

Everything you have is God's. God has been generous to you. Even if you are unsatisfied or hurt or living through a season of struggle, are you brave enough to believe that God has been generous to you even if you don't have everything you want?

He has, friend. It's all His. So be brave enough to steward everything you have in a way that displays God's great generosity.

Be Brave: *Make a list of all the gifts God has trusted you to steward—time, money, and so forth. No amount is too small. Look at all you have to offer the world!*

Day Eighty-One

BE GENEROUS WITH YOUR TIME

Share with the Lord's people who are in need. Practice
hospitality.

—ROMANS 12:13 NIV

For many years I was a volunteer leader for the college ministry
at my church. Each Sunday night after the service ended, we
would head to the gym together and eat cereal. Yep, cereal.
College students totally dig it. It's hilarious. My job for a while was
to oversee the cereal table.

This was my favorite time of the Sunday-night events. I got to
talk to every student and connect with them week after week. As
silly as it sounds, this was a big part of my ministry, and I loved it.

Maybe you're thinking, *Okay, Annie . . . but don't church tithes
go toward paying people to oversee the cereal tables?*

Yes, church staff members who give all their time to serving in
ministry love the ministry, but they do get paychecks so they can
live. But you know why I did it? Because this time I've been given is

not mine. God trusts me to be brave and to be generous with each day He gives me on this planet.

Could I have used the time I usually spent serving cereal to be doing something for my career or getting a mani-pedi? Sure I could. But I want to use God's time in a way that shows His love to others.

And it brought me so much joy. Giving my time to show hospitality to people in need . . . there's just no better way I could think of to spend my spare time.

This time I've been given it's not mine.

God exists outside of time. Isn't that crazy? He doesn't exist in our little timeline, and the time He's given us was created by Him and belongs to Him. So, listen, friend: if God's been generous to you, be brave enough to be selfless and generous with your time.

I know you can.

The enemy wants you to believe that your time is so precious that you need to conserve it to serve yourself. But serving other people, leading a small group, talking to your neighbor, whatever it is—that time is precious and that time is sacred, and God can love people supernaturally when you give them your time.

It's not easy to give your time to others. I get that. But when uncomfortable situations show up and keep you from doing what you want to do, are you brave enough to be generous with your time, trusting that God has a purpose in it?

Be Brave: *Take an hour this week and serve someone else.*

Day Eighty-Two

BE GENEROUS WITH YOUR WISDOM

If any of you lacks wisdom, let him ask God, who gives generously to all without reproach, and it will be given him.

—JAMES 1:5 ESV

So there it is: the Bible tells us, flat out, that if we want wisdom and we ask God for it, He's going to give it to us generously. *Generously.*

God is so generous with us. He gives good gifts to His children. And wisdom is such an incredible gift—it's all that Solomon asked Him for, and God told Solomon he could ask for *anything* (2 Chronicles 1:7)!

So listen. This is where your bravery comes in. You've been given wisdom by God, liberally. (If you haven't, ask Him for it!) Brave people offer their wisdom liberally to others. (Not opinions. *Wisdom.*)

A lot of people get hung up and think, *What wisdom do I have to offer? I'm only twenty!* Or *I've only been a Christian for a year. Surely there are better people to share their wisdom.*

Listen, friend. You *always* know more than someone else. Always.

There's always someone.

You may have been a Christian for only three days, but there's someone who will decide tomorrow to follow Jesus. Seriously. So you always have something to offer. Are you brave enough to believe that? Brave enough to share your wisdom?

Brave people offer their wisdom liberally to others. (Not opinions. Wisdom.)

I hope you remember this: the road to courage is lit by God's wisdom. His Word in the Bible and through the Holy Spirit to you and through others is how you see that road. You tap into that. You ask for that. You dig into that.

He will give you wisdom, and you can give it to others. You, friend, are qualified to share godly wisdom because you have God.

You can be brave enough to believe that. I know you can. And you can be brave enough to share it. Maybe with someone younger than you. A sibling. A cousin who wants advice. Or maybe it's someone older than you who is new in his or her faith. Ask God to give you opportunities to share wisdom with others today.

Be Brave: *Ask God for wisdom in your life. (This is something I pray for every single day.) And take some time today to thank someone who has been a wise voice in your life.*

Day Eighty-Three

>>>>———

BE GENEROUS WITH
YOUR MONEY

"No one can serve two masters, for either he will hate the one and love the other, or he will be devoted to the one and despise the other. You cannot serve God and money."

—MATTHEW 6:24 ESV

I will never forget the tsunami that hit Southeast Asia in 2004. I was a teacher at the time, and we were out of school for Christmas break. When we returned, the students in my class had many questions and a desire to do something to help.

Through the Red Cross, we found that we could donate money to provide people shelter and food. So we started a change drive. Kids from all over our school would bring change and drop it in a jar. On Fridays we would bring the jar to our room and pour the money out onto the floor. One table of students collected quarters, another dimes, another nickels, and another pennies. Then they would roll the coins.

Would you believe that in a single month we raised more than $1,000? (And not one cent was pocketed by my students.) We were able

Are you using your money in a way that honors Him?

to provide more than twenty family-sized tents for people in Asia. When the change drive began, I would not have believed that we would have that outcome, especially when twenty-five fifth graders were leading the charge. But with their sweet hands, they collected change, rolled coins, and wrote notes to send home to parents all over our school. They were servants. And God was honored by their offering.

Jesus said you can't serve God and money. It just doesn't work. You might think you don't love money more than God, but where is your money going?

Are you using your money in a way that honors Him? In a way that serves His people? Are you being irresponsible with your money and living off credit cards?

God blesses us when we give our tithes and offerings to Him. He uses our money to spread His love to others, and He blesses us so richly when we are generous.

It's not easy. I know! But are you brave enough to believe that if you are generous with your money, you won't run out?

Walk in obedience to God's Word, and be generous with your money. Take that brave step today and see how God blesses others—and you—through it.

BE BRAVE: *Give a little money away today—to a church, an organization, a friend, or a group you believe in.*

Day Eighty-Four

>>>>———————

BE GENEROUS WITH
YOUR WORDS

Gracious words are like a honeycomb, sweetness to the
soul and health to the body.

—PROVERBS 16:24 ESV

Brave people take God's Word and speak love into the lives of
others. Brave people let God love them and know they are
equipped for all the ways to use their words to speak love.

Today's verse is so beautiful and so true. Have you ever been
around someone whose words just grate? We can use our words to
hurt others, to be negative, to gossip, and to complain.

Or we can be brave enough to step out into a negative, cynical
world, where people want to hear gossip and negativity, and instead
we can be generous with our words and use them to bring life.

If we are focused on that—if our goal, day in and day out, is to be
generous and gracious, speaking love with our words—our negative
mind-sets and habits will fall away. The cussing will stop because it
doesn't fit into who you want to be. The sarcasm will slow because

you can't imagine hurting someone else with your words, even if it is unintentional. The inappropriate jokes may still come into your mind but not so much out of your mouth.

When we put God's Word in, diligently and routinely, the lesser things fall away. God makes us new, again and again, and we can be intentional and generous with our words to ourselves, to each other, and to God.

Brave people speak love into the lives of others.

I hope today that you will write a note. To anyone. To people who need some words of life poured into their hearts. I hope that you will stand up for people who can't stand up for themselves. And I hope you will think before you speak, choosing words that are gifts of light, not ones that cause death.

Friend, be brave. Be different in a world that uses words to hurt. Use your words to heal, and use them often. Give those words of life, the words found in Scripture, to as many people as you can.

Be Brave: *Write a note to someone you love who has been important to you lately. If you can, put it in the mail so he or she gets a good piece of surprise snail mail!*

Day Eighty-Five

>>>>————

BE GENEROUS WITH
YOUR HOME

Make sure you don't take things for granted and go slack in
working for the common good; share what you have with
others. God takes particular pleasure in acts of worship—a
different kind of "sacrifice"—that take place in kitchen and
workplace and on the streets.

—HEBREWS 13:16 MSG

*B*ill was the first man I ever loved. He was a tall, blond sixteen-
year-old. I was three. He was shy and quiet, but he always
talked to me. And he listened because I was then, as I am
now, a talker. He loved sitting beside me at dinner. He never missed
a family party. For my third birthday he gave me a plastic camera—
the flash was a small, multicolored cube on the corner of the camera
that turned when you pushed the button.

I was sure he was the coolest person who had ever existed on
earth. Bill was my dad's little brother in the Big Brothers Big Sisters
program through the Boys and Girls Club in our town.

I have so many clear memories of Bill. Dad would pick him up and bring him to our house a few times a month, and he would hang out for the day or stay for the weekend.

I remember where he was sitting on the couch when I opened that birthday gift, and I can still see his face as he smiled and laughed when I took his picture with my plastic camera with the click-and-turn flash. There was no film in the toy, but he never let on that he knew that.

Dad knew Bill for a long time, since Dad had been partnered with Bill since he was eight years old. But for being the first man I ever loved, I did not get enough time with Bill. Around Christmas in 1983, Bill was killed in a car accident. We returned home from a family Christmas event with my mother's family in Macon, Georgia, and my dad's father was waiting for us in the driveway. I can still see Grandpa Jack through the windshield, standing by his car, waiting to break the news to my dad.

Dad taught me a lesson with Bill, in his life and in his death, that he has continued to teach me over and over for my entire life: be brave enough to love the people around you, even if it could look like sacrifice and could feel like loss.

My parents welcomed Bill into our home. Again and again. They treated him like family. And you know what? We lost him. And hearts broke.

But while Bill was on earth, we shared our home and our family with him.

For many, home is a sanctuary. It's a place you go to retreat from a world that can be so harsh and so dark. And being generous with your home isn't easy. You might just want to be by yourself. You might not want to share your time. You might even be afraid that you'll get attached and then lose the person you've welcomed, like we did with Bill.

But brave people recognize that they can use their home to love others with the love of Christ. Brave people are generous with their homes. Brave people share—even their sanctuaries—with others.

Whether that looks like letting people live with you or letting people come over for dinner, you've got this!

Being generous with your home isn't easy.

When I was growing up, especially when I was in college, there was a family who made me feel like I could always come over. You know what? I felt like I had another home. They modeled for me that you don't have to hold everything so tightly. You don't have to live like that. Be generous with your home.

BE BRAVE: *Invite someone over to eat dinner at your house. Let him or her live in your family for a bit and be seen and cared for.*

Day Eighty-Six

WHAT YOU HAVE SHOULD AFFECT WHERE YOU ARE

Tell them to go after God, who piles on all the riches we could ever manage—to do good, to be rich in helping others, to be extravagantly generous. If they do that, they'll build a treasury that will last, gaining life that is truly life.

—1 TIMOTHY 6:18–19 MSG

Brave people deny themselves and serve others. Brave people are the ones who take what God's given them and give generously. Friend, your resources should make an impact wherever you go.

Your time. Your money. Your talents.

Serve someone else this week with your hands. Allow the Lord to lead you to those who could use a loving touch, and hug them.

The people you hug and touch and love this week can be changed because you hugged them and showed them the love of Christ in a tangible way.

Your home should be different because you're in it. You can look around at your family and the walls that hold you and see that place as a mission field. See your home as a place where you can love and you can forgive and you can make a difference.

I'll tell you a secret. (And if this gets out, I'll know exactly where it came from.) I'm a pretty selfish person. Some people on this earth are natural servants. They immediately think of other people first, volunteer whenever possible, and somehow have a smile on their faces for most of it. If that's you, I congratulate you. (And I humbly request that you teach me how to be like you.) But that isn't me. I have to choose to work at and focus on caring for other people more than I care about myself.

Your resources should make an impact wherever you go.

Because I want the places I go to be touched by God's love.

Your financial resources, however large or small, should be making a difference in this world—by furthering God's kingdom.

Give, friends. Be brave enough to put yourself, your wants, your money, and your time second place, so that what you have—what God's given you to steward—makes a difference wherever you go.

BE BRAVE: *Make a list of the ways you want to be courageously generous.*

Brave Enough to Be Where You Are

Be present right where you are.

Day Eighty-Seven

SACRED PLACES

"Do not come any closer," God said. "Take off your sandals,
for the place where you are standing is holy ground."

—Exodus 3:5 NIV

Throughout the Old Testament, we see places where God goes,
and those places are sacred. Moses had to take off his sandals
to be in God's presence.

But we have Jesus. The Holy Spirit lives in us. We aren't bound
by Old Testament laws anymore. We don't have to go into a taber-
nacle to be with God. We don't have to take off our shoes. We can
just talk to Him when we're in our beds or painting our nails or
folding laundry or typing numbers into a spreadsheet.

Because we have this amazing access to the Father through
Jesus, it's easy to get complacent and forget that our God is holy and
deserves our awe.

Yes, we can talk to Him wherever, but I think it's really important to have a sacred place with Him too. If you don't, it's hard to be
intentional. I mean, we're humans, so we might forget that God is
God and we owe Him our reverence.

Do you have a spot in your home where you spend time with God?

For me, it's my swirly chair. It's khaki brown (almost looks like a muted gold), and it has these awesome black swirls. It looks like a normal beautiful chair, but to me? It's sacred. It's special.

It's where I go when I'm talking to God, when I'm reading His Word, when I'm seeking Him.

Now, it's not the *only* place I go, but it's a special place.

Brave people are intentional people, and you've got to be intentional about your time with the Lord. You can't expect to be brave without spending time with Him—which is the whole reason you can be brave.

Yes, we can talk to Him wherever, but I think it's really important to have a sacred place with Him too.

Find your sacred space. It doesn't have to be fancy. The swirls in your chair don't have to be made of actual gold. Just find a spot in your home and make it sacred.

BE BRAVE: *Do you have a sacred spot? Where is it? What does it mean to you? (If you don't have a spot that feels sacred to you, find one! Make one!)*

Day Eighty-Eight

BE PRESENT
WHERE YOU ARE

"My command is this: Love each other as I have loved you."

—JOHN 15:12 NIV

Missionary Jim Elliot said, "Wherever you are, be all there."

I think that's really important. Wherever you live, wherever you work, wherever you hang out, be all there. For me to do that, I have to put my phone down sometimes.

Have you done that lately? Just put your phone down and ignored it for a while?

Our culture suffers from this whole idea of "FOMO" or "fear of missing out."

We constantly check our smartphones. Facebook. Instagram. Twitter. E-mail. Text. We don't want to miss anything . . . but in some ways, when my face is in my phone, I think I'm actually missing everything.

God loves us so much that He gave us His everything, and He asks us to love others the way He loved us. Loving others means being present with them in their pain, being present with them in their joy. It means being all there.

Maybe you're not a big phone person. Maybe it's TV for you, or a good book. But you know the thing you turn to when you want to escape. Everyone needs some downtime, but don't make it a crutch anymore. Put it down.

Are you brave enough to believe that you're not missing out on something else? Are you brave enough to believe that wherever you are, you can be all there, and that is exactly where you're meant to be?

Loving others means being all there.

Because that's the truth.

Think about the people who exude the love of Jesus. When you talk to them, are they distracted? Are they multitasking? I bet they aren't. I bet they are all there with you. I bet they are actively listening and praying over you with specificity because they are brave enough to be present.

Today, be intentional about being present where you are.

BE BRAVE: *What if you just took a break from your phone for a few hours? Or a day? Put it down and walk away. Notice the twinge of pain that comes when you think you might be missing something, but also embrace it!*

Day Eighty-Nine

WHERE YOU MEET
WITH GOD

Let the heavens rejoice, let the earth be glad; let the sea
resound, and all that is in it. Let the fields be jubilant, and
everything in them; let all the trees of the forest sing for joy.

—Psalm 96:11–12 NIV

One morning my heart woke up before my mind did. And while
my brain was like, *Sister, keep sleeping!* my heart knew something was up. I've been me long enough to know when I'm
supposed to listen to that little nudge.

So I got up, laced up, walked to the water, and climbed Lifeguard
Tower 52 on Newport Beach in Southern California. I asked God
what was so important, assuming we must have something to dis-
cuss since I was clearly awake on purpose.

And it was nothing.

No agenda.

No topic.

It was just us.

Just sitting. Just being.

Just together.

I played some worship music, an album from Brian and Jenn Johnson, and tears sprang to my eyes. Because after all these years together, it sure is sweet that sometimes the Lord wakes me up just to hang out.

That morning I met with God in nature. His creativity in nature grows something in me deep down in my soul. I looked out at the endless ocean He made just by speaking it into existence, and I remembered how much He loves me.

His love makes me brave, and there is no place I love to meet with God more than sitting in His creation. Sitting in nature.

When I'm home I often go to Radnor Lake. It's beautiful there, and I just can't walk those trails without my heart worshipping.

Spending time in God's creation, in His presence, will make you brave. You can be brave because you're God's. Today, even if it's just stepping outside of your office building and sitting under a tree, spend time in creation and remember how loved you are and how brave you can be.

> *There is no place I love to meet with God more than sitting in His creation.*

BE BRAVE: *Purchase* After All These Years *by Brian and Jenn Johnson. You're going to love that album! Go outside, get in nature, and let the music play in your ears.*

Day Ninety

>>> ———

YOUR HOME

My friends, you were chosen to be free. So don't use your
freedom as an excuse to do anything you want. Use it as an
opportunity to serve each other with love.

—GALATIANS 5:13 CEV

The longer I live, the more I'm figuring out that courage often
looks like sacrifice and service. In the places where you find
the most comfort, you have to have a little extra something to
give there. Home is where we rest. Home is where we find peace, so
to give from there, to sacrifice in that place, is to sacrifice deeply. I
think it's brave.

I didn't have a place to live when I moved back to Nashville
from Scotland.

All my belongings were in a storage unit somewhere in west
Nashville, and I no longer had an address. It was Thanksgiving, and
I planned to find something around Christmas.

Before leaving Nashville the previous summer, I had joked with
my friends Luke and Heather about moving in with them when I
got back. Sometime in the fall, Luke Skyped me and said the joke

was an actual offer. I was welcome to stay with them for a couple of weeks while trying to find a place.

I interrupted their lives. I added an entire human to their two-human household. I needed a key and a bed and a bathroom and the Internet.

Coming home after being overseas for six months, I was worried about reverse culture shock. It's a real thing, y'all. Being surrounded by a foreign culture, attempting to make it your own, and then coming back home—it can cause a normally sane person to lose it a little bit.

(And I'm not normally sane. So you've gotta factor that in too.)

But living with Luke and Heather was the most comfortable, warmest, friendliest environment. We decorated the Christmas tree, dressed in sweats to the movies, and walked to dinner at Edley's, the new barbecue restaurant in the neighborhood. In fact, another friend, Adam, came to live with us too, so we became a little family of four for that holiday season.

I think Luke and Heather's sacrifice rescued me from the pain of readjusting to Nashville and America.

I truly do.

New Year's Day came, and I still hadn't found a place to live. Weeks had accidentally turned into months, and it wasn't until mid-February that I was packing my things and moving to a house just down the street.

Home is where we find peace, so to sacrifice in that place is to sacrifice deeply.

Luke and Heather never complained. We talked about it openly and honestly multiple times, but they just kept giving—their space, their time, their money, their hearts.

It's brave to let a person live in your house who isn't your family.

How can you be brave in your home with the people you live with? Will you invite someone to stay with you for a while? Are you brave enough to be kind to your spouse? Can you unload the dishwasher first? Can you always take the trash out even if someone else should be doing it? What does it look like to serve and be brave in your own home?

Are you brave enough to find your place, even if your place is right here? Even if your place is in your home?

BE BRAVE: *Thank God for your home, for the place you live, and ask Him how you can be brave with your house.*

Day Ninety-One

>>>> ————

YOUR NEIGHBORHOOD

"The second is this: 'Love your neighbor as yourself.' There
is no commandment greater than these."

—MARK 12:31 NIV

*J*esus said the second greatest commandment outside of loving
God was to love your neighbors. So here's my question: What if
Jesus really meant the people you live around?

We can absolutely take this verse to mean all other people, like our
neighbors overseas, our neighbors in the checkout line, and so forth.

But, friend, you've got actual neighbors—actual souls all around
you who need hope and need to know that hope is found in Jesus.

So who are these neighbors? They're the moms at the gym.
They're the people at your school. When you walk out your front door,
if you make a 360-degree circle, they're those people. Do you know
them? Who are they? What do they do for a living, and how are you
serving them and caring about them?

My dad lives out the belief that you should be concerned for the
people nearest to you.

One of my dad's best childhood friends raised three boys virtually alone. Every so often my dad would take the boys out to eat or take us over to hang out with them and play on the playground. Dad has done accounting work for families even when they couldn't afford the help or weren't able to pay him (though we did get some fresh garden produce a time or two as payment). Dad met with a friend of mine when she lost her job and didn't know what to do about her lack of income. (Did I mention my dad is supersmart and everyone wants his advice?)

You can be brave enough to see those people around you, rather than just passing by.

Dad serves our local community with his time, money, and wisdom. It would be easier to worry just about our family. Trust me: we give him plenty to worry about. Instead, he cares for lots of families and does whatever he can to help them. It would be easier to worry just about his own company, but he chooses to care about others and their livelihoods.

Marietta, Georgia, is better because my mom and dad live there.

How is your neighborhood different because you live in it? You can be brave enough to see those people around you, rather than just passing by. You can be brave enough to serve them and love them, and God will use you, friend. You will be living out your mission as a light in this dark world.

BE BRAVE: *Introduce yourself to a neighbor you don't already know. Make a new friend with someone who lives near you.*

Day Ninety-Two

>>>———→

YOUR CITY

"Also, seek the peace and prosperity of the city to which I have carried you into exile. Pray to the LORD for it, because if it prospers, you too will prosper."

—JEREMIAH 29:7 NIV

God has placed you in your city for a purpose. Even if you wish you lived somewhere else right now, even if you're on a military base just for a season, even if you have bigger dreams. So what does it look like to love the city you're in?

Why is *here* your spot on the map? Why have you chosen that town, of all the towns in the world, to be your home? Maybe you didn't pick it. Maybe it picked you. But you are there.

When you think about the puzzle of the person you are, the zip code on your mailing address is an important piece.

As a high school senior, I stood in the middle of the town square in Ciudad Cortes, Costa Rica, and shared the gospel through an interpreter, and yet one of my best friends from my high school in Georgia was not a believer, and I didn't even talk to him about Jesus.

Why does it sometimes take more courage to talk about Jesus

at home? Why am I more willing to sign up for a mission trip to Mexico than to serve the homeless in downtown Nashville?

Because being brave at home means serving.

When my small group of college students celebrated our one-year anniversary, we decided to serve.

We arrived in downtown Nashville and made our way to a large overpass where many people were gathered under the bridge.

A worship band was playing, using one of *What does it* those sound systems that kinda hurts my *look like to love* ears—like a traveling preacher from the *the city you're in?* 1980s would use. Homeless people sat in rows and rows of chairs, each with a plate of food on their lap as volunteers wove in and out and helped everyone get settled.

It happens every Tuesday night in our town. The Bridge's outreach ministry feeds homeless men, women, and children a huge and healthy meal, and then someone shares the story of how God has changed his or her life. As the people leave, they fill bags with fresh produce donated by local grocery stores.

My small group and I had never gone before, but our church goes once a month on Tuesday nights, so we knew it was a respected ministry to be involved with.

The girls were nervous and hovered close to me like chicks to a hen for the first few minutes. But then they just got in line with the other volunteers and started to serve. Carrying food. Helping others find a seat. Passing out fruits, veggies, or huge bags of bread at the end of the night. We were there for a few hours, but the experience stuck with all of us much longer.

It takes courage to serve in new places just down the street. I was so proud of my girls jumping right in and being part of an experience where they didn't know was going to happen.

You can be brave right here. Right in your city.

Be Brave: *Volunteer in your city. Serve the place where you live in some way.*

Day Ninety-Three

YOUR COUNTRY

Let every person be subject to the governing authorities.
For there is no authority except from God, and those that
exist have been instituted by God.

—ROMANS 13:1 ESV

'm writing this at a weird point in American history. Donald
Trump just got elected as president of the United States, and the
country is full of a lot of people who are unhappy about this.
(And many who are happy, to be fair.)

Some are unhappy because they didn't want him to be the president. Some voted for him, but only because they felt like they didn't
have a better choice. And even his supporters aren't totally over the
moon because they're dealing with outrage from the other side. No
one is terribly happy, it seems.

The nation is very split right now, but when we look to God's
Word, we see that brave people trust God with who is or isn't in
authority over them.

The day after Trump won, *Late Show* host Stephen Colbert said something like this: your country is like your family—you don't just get to leave when you're unhappy.

What does that mean for you? Are you an American who wishes your country were different? Or maybe you live in a country where Christians are outright persecuted?

Brave people trust God with who is or isn't in authority over them.

No matter what your country's government looks like right now, you can be brave in it.

What does it look like to be brave enough to stay or brave enough to respect your country even if you don't agree with everything your country's leadership is doing?

Being brave looks like prayer. It looks like praying for your leaders to come to Christ. It looks like loving the people in your country and sticking to your biblical values.

No matter what the political state of things may be as you read this book, you can be brave in it. Carry on, friend.

Be Brave: *Pray for the leadership of your country.*

Day Ninety-Four

THE WORLD

And [Jesus] said to them, "Go into all the world and pro-
claim the gospel to the whole creation."

—MARK 16:15 ESV

Have you ever been on a mission trip? Have you ever left your
home country to tell other countries about Jesus?

If you haven't, I strongly suggest you do. You need to see
other places in the world because you need to see how they view God.

Living in every city on earth are people. Men and women like
you. Guys like your brother. Parents like your best friend's. Teachers
like the one who gave you an A in chemistry even when you probably
didn't deserve it. Almost seven billion people live on the earth right
now. Every day about 350,000 babies are born. That's about half the
population of the whole state of Alaska. That's a lot of people. Every
single person has a name. A face. A heart that needs to hear the
good news about Jesus.

I don't care if you go on a mission trip for six days or six
months—when you go into the world, you are trading your life for a
foreign life. And that takes courage.

If we want to see God glorified all over the world, we need to be brave enough to see courage in all its forms. And we need to do *the thing*. I can't see into your life to tell you what that thing is today. But I know enough to understand that the brave decisions you make at fifteen affect the brave choices you make at twenty-five—and they are different from the brave moments you face at thirty-five and fifty-five.

You need to see that the world is big and diverse.

If you've never gone, go. If you've never had a moment when no one around you speaks your language or shares your pigment or knows how elementary school works, you need to go. You *need* that. You need to see that the world is big and diverse, and maybe God doesn't look or sound the way you always thought He did because the world has a lot of different-looking and different-sounding people, all of whom are made in His image.

Save your money. Raise money. Connect with a mission-sending organization or a nonprofit organization. Be brave enough to send that first e-mail that says, "Can I go to Africa with you?" or "Yes, I'd like to be on that mission team to Mexico."

Do whatever it takes to expand your map. Because if you go where you've never gone before, you will see God like you've never seen Him before.

BE BRAVE: *Consider going on a mission trip with your local church or a mission organization like YWAM.*

Day Ninety-Five

>>>> ——————

JERUSALEM

Pray for the peace of Jerusalem: "May those who love you be secure. May there be peace within your walls and security within your citadels."

—PSALM 122:6–7 NIV

I've been to Jerusalem twice, and I absolutely love the city—both the old parts and the newer parts. It feels sacred. It feels as old as it is, and yet it feels like something fresh is stirring. The food is delicious; the cobblestone streets are lined with history that really matters; the shop owners are friendly. It's a beautiful place.

And Jesus was there.

God tells us about this city all throughout the Bible. He tells us to pray for the peace of Jerusalem. Jerusalem is the *only* city God specifically asks us to pray for.

So we shall. We are asked by God to pray for the peace of Jerusalem.

In Genesis 12, God promised blessings on those who bless Israel and curses on those who curse her.

Besides Jerusalem being the holy land and the center of Jewish life, Jerusalem is prophesied to be the scene of Christ's return in Acts 1:11 and Zechariah 14:4.

Prayer is our most direct connection to God—your voice to His ear. I don't have any special insider information on prayer. I don't understand why it seems to "work" sometimes and then not work other times. I can list for you many prayers I've uttered throughout the years that I don't understand what God did with them.

Jerusalem is the only city God specifically asks us to pray for.

We've talked about the power of prayer and, y'all, it is real. Prayer changes things.

So when you pray for places like your home and your neighborhood and your city and your country and the world, pray for Jerusalem. Pray for the bravery of those who are being persecuted for their beliefs. Pray for a revival. Pray.

BE BRAVE: *Add Jerusalem to your list of prayers. Pray for the peace of Jerusalem.*

BRAVE ENOUGH

Brave choices always have ripple effects.

Day Ninety-Six

JESUS WAS BRAVE

"If the world hates you, keep in mind that it hated me first."
—JOHN 15:18 NIV

As I am now in my midthirties, Jesus and I have lived on earth about the same amount of time, give or take. It's crazy to think about. We both lived through our twenties—He with no mistakes or regrets, me with enough for both of us. Something gets very real about Jesus being human when you are the same age as He was.

When you *only* think about Jesus as divine, then you sort of miss the fact that Jesus is human. So when my mind and heart began to reflect on the two natures a bit, everything changed.

I realized just how brave Jesus was. He walked away from a job that was stable. He walked away from a respectable life to become homeless and to roam around Israel for three years talking about the kingdom of God.

I can't imagine my friends turning on me the way Peter turned on Jesus. I can't imagine church leaders hating me the way they hated Jesus. I can't imagine being brave in all the ways He was. I can't imagine not knowing Him. I'm so glad I get to. Something changed the closer I got to His age. I started to know Him differently. I saw Him like one of my friends, like one of the dudes I hang with all the time. He's not some adult doing adult things; He's my age.

It stokes my fire of courage, remembering that Jesus did some majorly brave things right here—right where I am. Single like me. Human like me. Sinless, unlike me, but tempted like me. And He took a risk on me.

The world hated Jesus, but He was brave enough to give His life for it anyway.

He asked His disciples to do the same. To give up everything to follow Him, and He asks us to do the very same thing. To follow Him. To live our lives bravely, as He lived His—pouring it out for a hurting, hostile world. The world hated Jesus, but He was brave enough to give His life for it anyway. What love.

The truth of who Jesus is and what He did on earth—the Son of God who came to earth to take on our sins—is the most courageous thing this planet has ever seen.

BE BRAVE: *Thank Jesus for the courage He showed in all the Bible stories you have read about Him.*

Day Ninety-Seven

JESUS IS BRAVE

Then I saw heaven opened, and behold, a white horse! The one sitting on it is called Faithful and True.

—REVELATION 19:11 ESV

*D*id you just read this verse? That hasn't happened yet. You realize that, right? Jesus is coming back, not as the baby in the humble manger, but as the mighty King of kings and Lord of lords.

Baby Jesus was brave. But Baby Jesus was here on a mission to save us from our sin. He's already done that good work. He's already died and resurrected.

Jesus is still alive and still working for our good today. He is still the humble King who came to earth, but His mission will be different when He returns. He's going to come back and judge sin once and for all and destroy the enemy who has made this world such a broken and painful place.

See, Jesus wasn't just brave in the past tense. Jesus is brave today.

Jesus knows I'm a screwup, and for that, He gave His life. I am so grateful for that salvation. But over and over again, I ask Jesus for forgiveness and rescue, and He always provides them. You would never buy a car that got a flat tire every time you test-drove it, and you would stop eating at restaurants that repeatedly got your order wrong. And yet Jesus does that for me all the time. I have a flat tire and get His order wrong and sin and everything in between. He takes risks for me, and He takes a risk on me.

He is still the humble King who came to earth, but His mission will be different when He returns.

John 3:16 says it all. God loves you so much that He gave up His own Son so that your sin would not be able to separate you from Him forever. God is holy and we are sinners. But Jesus bridged that gap; His death and resurrection cleared that path.

His resurrection proved that He is God—that He has the power to overcome death and that His forgiveness of our sins was real!

He deeply loves you and deeply knows you and is doing the hard work of forgiving and forgiving and forgiving again and again. Jesus *is* brave, and He made you to be brave too.

BE BRAVE: *Thank Jesus that He takes a risk on you over and over again. Thank Him that the grave did not hold Him down and that He is a risen and living King.*

Day Ninety-Eight

YOU WERE MADE TO BE BRAVE

Then David said to Solomon his son, "Be strong and courageous and do it. Do not be afraid and do not be dismayed,
for the LORD God, even my God, is with you. He will not
leave you or forsake you, until all the work for the service of
the house of the LORD is finished."

—1 CHRONICLES 28:20 ESV

What a great father-son speech we see in 1 Chronicles 28.
Truth being passed down from dad to kid.

That's what the Bible does for us, you know. We read
the Bible, and it's just like our Dad is talking to us. And He's saying
exactly what David said to Solomon.

*Hey, you! Hey, kid! Be strong! Have courage. Why? Because I'm
with you.*

He's with you, friend. Do you see that now? You are two days
away from being finished with *100 Days to Brave*. Two.

Do you see how brave God has made you? Jesus was brave,

through and through. Jesus is brave. And we see Him modeling it for us, from the way He lived His life on earth to the way He loves us today.

There is not an area of your life that can't be touched and improved by courage. When you look back at the time you've spent in this book and in God's Word, do you see that?

Courage isn't just for mighty warriors. It's for you (because you are becoming courageous). It's for your relationship with God. It's for your dreams and your calling and your work. It's for your relationships with fellow humans.

Courage isn't just for mighty warriors. It's for you (because you are becoming courageous).

You can be brave during all the changes of life. You can be brave in the face of pain. You can be brave with your health. Brave with your money. Brave wherever you are!

Your God will not leave you or forsake you. And because you know that, you are brave.

Be Brave: *What's the biggest change you see in your life over the past few months?*

Day Ninety-Nine

>>>>———

YOU ARE BRAVE

Take a good look at God's wonders—they'll take your breath away.

—PSALM 66:5 MSG

R emember back in Day 3 of this book? You probably don't. It was a long time ago. Look how long you've been brave with me! Wow.

So back in Day 3, I was telling you about my move to Nashville and how unbrave I felt as I took brave steps.

I told you—I never *felt* brave. I never had a moment of extreme courage or belief that this was going to be the best decision I had ever made. I just kept on doing the next thing God had for me.

When you started this 100-day journey, I bet you were challenging yourself, taking brave steps, and all the while feeling terrified. But look back, friend. Flip through these pages and look at how brave you are.

You were always brave. I knew that. But you may not have felt brave.

Do you see now? Do you see that you are braver than you know?

You have lived some of your dreams. You've done the hard work of loving others sacrificially.

You've even chosen to add more vegetables to your life. I'm proud of you for that. Today you are braver than you thought you were when you cracked open this book for the first time.

I am so proud of you.

I want you to take this day to reflect on what God has done. Reflect on the awesome miracles He has performed for you and in you and in the people around you.

Your brave choices have ripple effects. Brave people inspire those around them to be brave.

You were always brave. I knew that. But you may not have felt brave.

And you know you, just like I know me. All glory for any bravery we exhibit goes straight to Jesus. He is the brave One. He made us. He created and modeled brave. And here we are at the end of our journey, but the start of a new mind-set.

You are braver than you know.

Be Brave: *Take that dry-erase marker that you keep in your bathroom now, and write this on the mirror: "I am braver than I realize. And I will prove it today."*

Day One Hundred

LET'S ALL BE BRAVE

"The LORD your God is with you, the Mighty Warrior who saves. He will take great delight in you; in his love he will no longer rebuke you, but will rejoice over you with singing."

—ZEPHANIAH 3:17 NIV

If you follow me on social media or if you've brushed by me in a craft store, you know how much I love glitter and sparkly things, mainly confetti poppers.

I love them because they're happy and pretty and celebratory and awesome, but also because they remind me why it's so important for me to be brave. Here's why: because my courage affects other people the same way that my being near you with a confetti popper will make your life different and better and more amazing.

Your courage affects other people, and it's just like that confetti popper. When you pull that string off with courage and you celebrate with sparkles, other people will feel like they can get confetti all over the place too.

They'll see you and be like, "I want to do that!"

Making brave choices in your life is going to change the world.

At the least, it will change *your* world. But I dare not limit what you are going to do on this planet, friend. Your life is Jesus' reward for His suffering—your brave yeses, your courageous noes, hanging on, letting go, going there, staying here, all of it.

> *Making brave choices in your life is going to change the world. At the least, it will change your world.*

I hope you've already done it. I hope you've already taken that first step because I am sure, like I've rarely been so sure of anything before, that your people are waiting and your God is watching with expectancy for you to see where your map is going to take you.

And today I pray peace for you.

And joy. And hope. And courage—the deep, deep kind that changes the way you live.

Instead, hold your map and the hand of your Father. And let's all be brave.

BE BRAVE: *I think you probably need to go buy a confetti popper. Then take a picture of yourself shooting it into the air! Post the picture online and include the hashtag #100daystobrave.*

Thank You

First of all, to you, my reader friend, thank you for walking this entire road with me. It means more than you can know. I've thought about you every day of writing and editing and planning and dreaming. This was always for you.

Writing this book, taking some most beloved pieces and adding them to new worked-up words, took a lot of people. I'm so lucky to get to work with this team at HarperCollins Christian Publishing. Laura, Molly, Carly—y'all are the best. Thank you, Scarlet Hiltibidal, for all your hours with me and these words. Dawn Hollomon, you did the hard work of editing this with me, and I'll be forever grateful for all the ways it is the best book because of you. Tim, Hannah, Stefanie, Michael—thank you for helping this book get into the hands of as many of my friends as possible. From the cover design (Adam, you are my hero) to the layout of the words to the prayers lifted, I'm so thankful I don't have to do this alone.

Thank you to Lisa Jackson for making this all work so smoothly and to Katie and Eliza and April (and Haile!) for running things at Downs Books Inc. when I'm smothered in words on pages. To them and to the rest of my team— Brian, Heather, Becky, Brian, Emily, Kelli, Chad, Leigh, Shaun, Patrick—I am a sinking ship without you. Thanks for being my sails.

To my family and friends, my people, the ones who put up with this crazy, unexpected life that is mine, thank you for being here.

To Jesus. You saved me once, but You rescue me all the time. When I feel like I'm looking so hard for You in all these pages, in my story and life, in the places I'm asking these reader friends to be brave, I'm thankful You always show up. I'm thankful You are not hard to find. You make me brave, and I'll love You forever for it.